T0323747

Body Care

Richard Templar

■ Fast track route to improving the health of your organization and yourself

■ Covers key health management techniques, from eliminating stress to auditing diet, and from positive self-expression to maintaining a healthy work-home balance

■ Packed with lessons and bodycare tips

■ Includes a glossary of key concepts and a comprehensive resources guide

essential management thinking at your fingertips

LIFE & WORK

10.07

First published 2002 by
Capstone Publishing (a Wiley company)
8 Newtec Place
Magdalen Road
Oxford OX4 1RE
United Kingdom
http://www.capstoneideas.com

CIP catalogue records for this book are available from the British Library and the US Library of Congress

ISBN 1-84112-392-7

This book is printed on acid-free paper

Substantial discounts on bulk quantities of Capstone books are available to corporations, professional associations and other organizations. Please contact Capstone for more details on +44 (0)1865 798 623 or (fax) +44 (0)1865 240 941 or (e-mail) info@wiley-capstone.co.uk

Contents

Introduction to ExpressExec

ExpressExec is 3 million words of the latest management thinking compiled into 10 modules. Each module contains 10 individual titles forming a comprehensive resource of current business practice written by leading practitioners in their field. From brand management to balanced scorecard, ExpressExec enables you to grasp the key concepts behind each subject and implement the theory immediately. Each of the 100 titles is available in print and electronic formats.

Through the ExpressExec.com Website you will discover that you can access the complete resource in a number of ways:

» printed books or e-books;
» e-content – PDF or XML (for licensed syndication) adding value to an intranet or Internet site;
» a corporate e-learning/knowledge management solution providing a cost-effective platform for developing skills and sharing knowledge within an organization;
» bespoke delivery – tailored solutions to solve your need.

Why not visit www.expressexec.com and register for free key management briefings, a monthly newsletter and interactive skills checklists. Share your ideas about ExpressExec and your thoughts about business today.

Please contact elound@wiley-capstone.co.uk for more information.

10.07.01

Introduction to Body Care

» A healthy workforce means a healthy organization;
» work-related health is closely linked to personal health and to health in the home;
» body care is holistic: the parts of the body all depend on one another and when one part suffers ill health, the whole body is affected;
» some work practices, such as computer use, create a need for a very specific kind of body care;
» environmental body care;
» personal body care programs;
» resources and terminology;
» disclaimer: this is not a diagnostic book.

"A healthy workplace ... it's money in the bank."
Canadian Institute for Work and Health, "How the workplace can influence employee illness and injury," Robson L., Polanyi M., Kerr M., & Shannon H. (1998)

Many companies have recently realised that improving the health of their workforce is a sound financial investment. And it is. This book is about doing exactly that – improving body care. But there are considerations beyond mere money. This book takes a two-pronged approach to body care and health care. The first is about the financial savings that can be made, and the greater efficiency that can be achieved, by maintaining a healthy workforce: it makes sense not to have extreme absenteeism and a high turnover of staff. Healthy bodies house healthy minds. The second aspect is personal health care – taking responsibility for your own health and looking after yourself beyond the level that your employing organization is prepared to offer you.

AN HOLISTIC APPROACH

Body care looks at the *whole* body – muscles, digestive system, heart and lungs, immune system, nervous system, everything that keeps us alive – and what we can do to both prevent the onset of detrimental conditions and maintain and improve our basic health and body care. Obviously we cannot separate the mind from the body, and conditions such as stress, although their primary effect is mental, do have their physical symptoms and indicators. We have to have an holistic approach to see how the entire system fits together, to understand the relationship between different parts of the body, and to devise ways in which the body can be made to function better.

Body care at home

For good body care to work, we have to devise and implement programs that carry over from our workplace into our home life as well. Although this book is designed specifically for work-related problems that affect our bodies, it is important to realize that we do not leave our bodies behind when we leave the office or the factory at the end of the working day. We take them with us everywhere, and what we implement at work for good body care will have ramifications for good body care at home as well. And obviously the opposite is true; stress, poor diet, lack of exercise, and poor sleeping patterns at home will affect our body care at work. We have to find the right balance between work and home for our bodies to operate at their best in both environments.

Healthier is happier

Research has shown that healthier employees are more productive, take less time off for sickness, and are more resilient to stress and problems. And healthier employees tend to stay longer in a job – they are happier as well as healthier, and their work benefits accordingly.

Computer-related strain

Body care is not just about taking enough exercise, or eating a nutritional and balanced diet. It is also about preventing our bodies from having to undergo stresses and strains that they are not equipped to bear. Most of us have to sit still at keyboards for long hours, with our limbs in unnatural and often unsupported positions and our eyes focused on something which is unnaturally close; we shall look in Chapter 4 at the problems which can be created by visual display units (VDUs), such as eyes train, headaches and backache.

A personal body care program

We shall also look at setting up a body care program in the workplace for employees – what the employer is legally and morally bound to provide in terms of health and safety features – and how to set up a personal body care program.

Environmental body care

It is not too long ago since our ancestors thought nothing of sending small boys up chimneys, since women and children considered themselves fortunate to get work in coal mines, and since employers expected workers to suffer industrial hazards and dangerous conditions without complaint and without any access to legal protection. We shall also look at environmental body care, and consider what individuals can do for themselves in order to avoid being affected by work-related hazards.

RESOURCES

Good body care is ongoing – it is not simply a matter of spending a week or two practicing good body care and then expecting it to last a year – so Chapter 9 contains information on the best resources available. This includes where to go for advice both as an individual and as a team leader promoting good body care for yourself and for your team members. The resources listed include Websites, books, magazines, and government information booklets and leaflets.

THE TEN STEP PROGRAM FOR PERSONAL BODY CARE

Chapter 10 outlines a simple Ten Step program for maintaining good body care and avoiding future problems. This is a simple but highly effective program, designed to be carried out quickly and successfully.

THE TERMINOLOGY WE USE

Before we can maintain the machine – your body – we have to know how it works. Chapter 2 – What is Body Care? – outlines the terminology we shall be using throughout the book, what each part of the body needs in the way of good health, and what sort of methods are available to correct problems, such as the Alexander Technique, osteopathy, acupuncture and acupressure, massage and aromatherapy, relaxation and meditation techniques, counselling and therapy, and yoga. Chapter 8 defines these and other terms related to body care. The more open-minded we are about adopting techniques from disciplines outside our normal range of experience, the more benefit we can gain. To maintain physical well-being we have to be vigilant and prepared to change. We have to listen to what out bodies are telling us and not rely solely on a body care regime that is too inflexible. We have to monitor what is happening to our bodies on a day-to-day basis, and be prepared to change what we are doing to improve and enhance our body care.

DISCLAIMER

This book is designed to provide information about body care. It is not designed to be used in any way for diagnostic purposes. If you are in any doubt about any condition you may be suffering from, then consult a qualified medical practitioner immediately. ExpressExec can accept no responsibility for misdiagnosis or wrong treatment for any condition. This book provides information only, and for general purposes only.

Definition of Terms:
What is Body Care?

» What will we put up with?
» working to live, living to work;
» practical solutions – setting standards for good body care;
» preventing heart disease;
» efficient lung use;
» circulation – recognizing the symptoms of poor circulation;
» brain and mind – the mind/body relationship;
» the skeletal system – bones, muscles, joints, back, and neck;
» the immune system – our defence against attack from infection;
» the holistic whole body approach – the fragile components;
» what can go wrong – RSI, depression, internal disorders, fatigue and exhaustion;
» putting it right – the Alexander Technique, chiropractic, counseling and therapy, kinesiology, massage and aromatherapy, osteopathy, relaxation and meditation, yoga.

WHAT WILL WE PUT UP WITH?

In order to enjoy full and complete body care, we have to know what we expect in the way of good health. Are we prepared to tolerate aches and pains? Do we expect to suffer backache from sitting too long in the same position? Should it be part of normal working life that we have to snatch quick snacks at lunchtime instead of eating a healthy and balanced nutritional meal? Are we really expected to suffer constant worry and put up with levels of stress that can become intolerable? There are no right or wrong answers – and we are all different in our levels of expectation and tolerance. Every individual must make a personal decision about how much he or she is prepared to tolerate, and then devise a lifestyle which accommodates that level of tolerance.

Work to live, live to work

Working to live, however, is infinitely preferable to living to work. We shall look later (in Chapter 5) at the work/home balance, but it is worth pointing out here that creating poor posture at work, or tolerating work-related stress that could be lessened or even eliminated, will inevitably have a detrimental effect on our home life.

PRACTICAL SOLUTIONS

If we experience poor body care at work, we carry the ramifications home with us and we pass the results on to our partner, to our families and to our friends. We have to set standards for good body care that are achievable, simple to carry out, and efficient. We need practical solutions and successful effective techniques. Reading about body care doesn't achieve anything – we have to *do* something as well. Let's have a quick guided tour of the machinery – your body – to see where the problem areas are and what sort of things can go wrong. There are six main areas of concern for the internal body – heart, lungs, circulation, brain, the musculoskeletal system, and the immune system. We can start with those.

The heart

Preventing heart disease starts with good body care practices. The heart is the most important organ in the body and requires the greatest care.

The heart is simply a very efficient pump. But it can get clogged up and fail to pump effectively. Fatty deposits known as *atheroma* can clog up the coronary arteries, cutting off the oxygen supply to the heart. When the arteries become partially clogged, a pain known as *angina* is caused; this is a severe warning sign that should not be ignored at any cost. Complete blockage of the arteries results in a heart attack *(myocardial infarction)* which is potentially and often fatal.

Drugs can be prescribed which open up the coronary arteries to provide pain relief from the angina but bypass surgery is ultimately the only recourse. This is severe and serious. Drugs can also be used to control high blood pressure after a heart attack and to regulate the heart itself. Again severe and serious. It is far better not to let the heart get into such a state in the first place. But what causes it? Research has shown that we can take sensible steps to address the main causes and to give ourselves a chance of avoiding such problems if we:

» cut down on the amounts of salt, sugar, and fat in the diet;
» maintain a healthy, balanced, and sensible diet (see Chapter 7);
» take half an hour of sustained, vigorous exercise twice a week;
» maintain a sensible weight in relation to body size;
» stop smoking; and
» have the blood pressure checked regularly.

We shall look at ways to aid you in all these later, in the section on setting up a personal body care program.

Researchers at the University of Michigan, widely reported in the press in January 2001, say that consuming plenty of folic acid – either as a supplement or in such foods as breakfast cereals, green vegetables and pulses – is the best way to reduce the risk of heart disease. Folic acid helps to cut down levels of homocysteine, an amino acid that clogs up the arteries and makes the blood more likely to clot. Vitamin B12, found in meat, eggs and dairy products, also helps.

The lungs

The lungs are the big bags located in the chest which fill up with air when we breathe in. They pretty well do their job all by themselves, don't they? Well, yes they do, but it is amazing how much we do to impede their work. Smoking is obviously the worst threat, but so is breathing other people's smoke. Breathing in polluted air is detrimental, and being stressed also causes our lungs to work inefficiently.

Once the smaller airways in the lungs (the *bronchioles)* start to get blocked, we can suffer asthma and the more serious disease of lung cancer. We need to look after our lungs if we are to maintain good body care and the three most effective steps we can take are:

» stop smoking;
» wear a mask if working in or passing through polluted atmosphere; and
» relax the whole body, so that the lungs have a chance to work effectively.

Circulation

Good circulation of the blood around the body is essential to good body care. The blood in the arteries carries not only oxygen and food, but also essential cells to fight off infection and repair damage. The main problem with arteries is that they can become clogged with a fatty deposit called *cholesterol*, so any steps you take to maintain good heart care will also have a positive effect on the circulation.

The arteries also work as a effective climate control system for the body, which is why you suffer from cold hands and feet in severe weather – the circulation is conserving what heat the body has for the heart, brain, and other vital organs.

One of the easiest symptoms of poor circulation to recognize is varicose veins, which are caused by the valves in the veins of the legs becoming weak and preventing efficient blood flow. Varicose veins are genetic – you are much more likely to get them if others in your family suffer from them – but also preventable and treatable. Much more serious is a clot in the veins (a *thrombosis*) which can break loose and travel to the lungs where it can be life-threatening. Watch out for warning signs such as pain in the legs, swellings, and/or discoloration. If you take a contraceptive pill and/or smoke, consult a qualified medical practitioner immediately if you suffer any of these symptoms.

To avoid varicose veins:

» maintain a sensible weight in relation to body size;
» avoid constipation – a common contributory factor – by eating a high fibre diet;

» avoid prolonged standing; and
» wear support hose if necessary.

Brain and mind

The brain is the body's control center, the seat of consciousness, the organizational linchpin in the whole machine. It is also a highly sensitive organ and is easily thrown off-balance. The brain/mind combination is easily disturbed by stress, anxiety, depression, and worry. It is also vulnerable to injury, and to internal attack from clots which can cause strokes. If we are to protect the brain and mind properly, we need to carry out all of the following precautions:

» avoid drugs, especially the hallucinogenic ones, and too much alcohol, all of which impair brain function;
» take regular exercise;
» take time to relax and switch off – avoid too much work;
» understand our own limits, and pay attention to any stresses and strains we feel threatened by;
» maintain regular and sufficient sleep patterns;
» be ready and prepared to talk about any feelings we have of low self esteem, inadequacy, stress, anxieties, worries, and any feelings of hopelessness or desperation; and
» maintain a balanced and regular diet, with an adequate supply of vitamin B (bananas, milk, mushrooms, nuts, oily fish).

Maintaining a healthy mind is essential to good body care. The mind is the personality's control centre and if it is affected in any way, it can influence the entire machinery. We must aim to achieve a balanced approach to life with plenty of enjoyment and satisfaction, and regular exercise and relaxation.

Musculoskeletal system

Bones, muscles, joints, back, and neck – these are what hold the body together and enable us to move, and they are all prone to disease, disaster, and bad body care. Joints suffer from osteo-arthritis which affects over three-quarters of people over 50. Muscles become over-stretched and painful. Back problems affect many of us; over a million people in the UK are kept away from work in any one week with back problems. Massage and complementary therapies can ease many of these conditions, and we shall look at them in more detail later in this chapter and in Chapter 8. Suffice it to say that the body needs regular attention and maintenance if it is to function properly and efficiently. Lack of maintenance, poor diet, and lack of exercise only escalate the problems.

Immune system

The immune system is a vital part of good body care. It defends us against attack from bacteria and viruses and also helps stop cancers from developing or spreading. Sometimes the immune system itself becomes defective and over-reacts causing such conditions as hay fever, eczema, and asthma. A strong, healthy body has a strong, healthy immune system. The healthier you are the greater the likelihood there is that you are able to fight off infection and disease. Again an holistic approach is needed as the immune system is dependent on a healthy mental approach, which in turn is engendered by a healthy body – which obviously needs a healthy immune system. We cannot treat any one part in isolation. Each part of the body is interdependent on all the others for efficient working. If any part is out of balance, the other parts will suffer. Keeping the immune system in top condition is vital and dependent on:

» a balanced and nutritional diet, containing a high proportion of fresh vegetables, fruit, and protein;
» not smoking, and avoiding too much alcohol;
» regular exercise;
» avoiding harmful stress – but this does not mean avoiding pressure, challenge stimulation, difficulties, or demands;
» an adequate daily intake of vitamins B, C and E, as well as iron – anti-oxidants have also been shown to boost our immune system; and
» avoiding antibiotics if we can "get better" without them in such conditions as flu.

By now you may have detected a pattern: in nearly all cases, the means necessary to avoid harming any of our organs or internal systems is the same – a good diet, regular exercise, avoiding too much alcohol and not smoking. But we all appreciate that all this is far from easy sometimes: this book will provide many practical hints and tips to make it easier.

The other parts of the body

So far in this chapter we have dealt with the major organs and systems that are likely to be affected by work-related problems. There are many other organs and systems which we trust will not be affected by work-related problems, such as the sexual organs, urinary system, stomach, and bowels. But we cannot afford to be too compartmental about functions such as these. Serious work stress can badly affect sexual performance. Poor diet at work can induce stomach ulcers and bowel disorders. Stress can have an effect on the ways in which any urinary infections clear up, and on how quickly we recover from a whole host of complaints and conditions.

THE WHOLE BODY APPROACH

We must regard the whole body as a single entity made up of many fragile and interdependent components – any of which can give trouble, cease to work effectively, or break down completely as a result of work-related problems. Some of the symptoms may only be revealed once we are at home or away from work. We might show signs only when we are at work, and be quite free from them at home – but this does not mean that the condition does not continue to affect us. Body care has to be an holistic study, and it has to take place away from work just as much as at work, although this book will concentrate on the sort of problems that work can induce, such as eye strain through too much VDU work.

WHAT CAN GO WRONG?

We have had a very brief look at the major parts of the body. Now we need to know what sort of thing can go wrong with them, and how to recognize it when it does. Work-related disorders tend to fall into four major categories:

» physical problems such as repetitive strain injury (RSI), eye strain, and back pain and disorders;

» mental problems such as depression, stress, and breakdown;
» internal disorders such as heart disease, immune system break-down, and hyperventilation (over-breathing brought on by stress); and
» general disorders such as fatigue, exhaustion, insomnia, and lack of appetite.

Most of these are stress-related and beyond the scope of this book, although we shall cover them in a general way. Detailed information on work-related stress is available in the ExpressExec book *Stress*; this will point you more than favorably in the right direction. But as we are adopting an holistic approach to body care, it is impossible to ignore the effects that stress has on the other major areas of problems.

Each of these four major categories of work-related disorders has its own warning symptoms, and it is advisable to monitor your own individual system to make sure everything is working well – see Chapter 7 for further information on self-analysis.

PUTTING IT RIGHT

Once the system starts to break down we have to take immediate remedial action to put things right. If the condition is serious enough to warrant taking time off work, or the intervention of a qualified medical practitioner, then obviously it is serious enough for us to be seeking outside help. But what can we do for ourselves? There is a whole range of therapies and disciplines that can offer considerable help in correcting work-related problems. These therapies and disciplines include:

» the Alexander Technique;
» chiropractic;
» counseling and therapy;
» kinesiology;
» massage and aromatherapy;
» osteopathy;
» relaxation and meditation; and
» yoga.

The Alexander Technique

Most people first experience the Alexander Technique with the help of a qualified teacher. The discipline was founded by Frederick Matthias Alexander around the end of the nineteenth century. Alexander was a Tasmanian actor who found that he had voice problems which cleared up when he adjusted his posture. His entire teachings are based on the fact that we unconsciously develop bad postural habits which feel familiar and right but are wrong. When we move, or are moved, into correct postures, they feel wrong because they are unfamiliar. The Alexander technique is about unlearning bad postural habits which are causing us muscular aches and joint pains.

Chiropractic

Chiropractic is a discipline founded towards the end of the nineteenth century by a Canadian, Daniel Palmer, who believed that since the nervous system is closely integrated with the skeletal system, any malfunction in one could be treated by manipulation of the other. Chiropractors place great importance on the spine and believe that most muscular aches and pains, back problems, joint pains, and sciatica can all be relieved by hands-on manipulation of the spine. Chiropractic is a very similar discipline to osteopathy but aims for much more long-term treatment of chronic back problems, whereas osteopathy tends to work on the short-term, more immediate treatment of specific conditions.

Counseling and therapy

Counseling and therapy are similar in their approach. They both involve face-to-face meetings with a qualified and trained practitioner, who encourages the patient to talk about his or her concerns and problems, and then helps the patient to come to terms with them. Counseling is usually effective in short-term disorders such as relationship break-downs, or in encouraging motivational skills and assertiveness. Therapy, usually in the form of psychotherapy, is for more long-term problems such as depression, anxiety attacks, fears, and phobias.

Kinesiology

Kinesiology is a relatively new therapy which was developed in the 1960s by an American chiropractor, George Goodheart, who discovered that muscle strength was reduced when the patients being tested were exposed to any substance they were allergic to. It is now used as a non-invasive method to test for dietary allergies, nutritional deficiencies, and emotional imbalances. It is also used to treat back pain, muscular tension, headaches and migraines, eczema, IBS (irritable bowel syndrome), and depression. Treatment is usually in the form of elimination diets to find out which foods are causing the problems.

Massage and aromatherapy

There are many different forms of massage, and aromatherapy is one that has been proved to be highly effective in relieving the symptoms of stress, tiredness, and tension, and in generally restoring the overall well-being of an individual. Massage can be used to relieve joint pain, ease muscular movements, ease stiffness, and relax tense muscles. It can also be very useful in treating injuries, especially sports injuries.

Osteopathy

Osteopathy was developed around 1870 by a physician, Andrew Taylor, who believed that muscular and skeletal disorders could cause illness and that the use of massage and manipulation could improve the working of joints and muscles. A trained osteopath will examine the spine to look for incorrect functioning and will manipulate the spine and joints to ease tissue pain and muscular problems. Osteopathy has been found to be beneficial in the treatment of high blood pressure, irritable bowel syndrome, headaches and migraines, and asthma.

Relaxation and meditation

Relaxation and meditation techniques are usually quick and easy to learn and can be practiced alone, at work and at home. They should not be complicated or overlaid with any belief system.

Yoga

Yoga is a philosophy, not a religion. It has many branches and types but the most important of these in the context of work-related body care is *hatha* yoga, which deals with physical health. This is not a short-term fix, but once it has been learnt – and is practiced on a daily basis – it will provide a lifetime physical fitness regime. It uses simple postures – *asanas* – which gently stretch both the body frame and the internal organs. Newcomers to yoga need about three months training before they can practice on their own.

So we have had a good look at the body and seen how easily it can go wrong as we go about our daily lives. We have also looked at some different forms of treatment. We do need to look at these, since conventional Western medicine may not have the answers, or the time, to deal with such work-related conditions. On the other hand, any serious symptoms of disease or illness should always be promptly reported to a qualified medical practitioner, just to be on the safe side. A doctor may prescribe painkillers for back problems but body care offers longer-term solutions – not just treating conditions but making sure that they do not recur. Prevention rather than cure. In the next chapter we shall look at the evolution of body care. It is a long time since small boys were being sent up chimneys and those days have gone. But how come we have all become so health conscious? Let's look at how, and why now.

The Evolution of Body Care

The factors which have influenced the evolution of body care:

» litigation – taking employers to court, compensation, reporting serious symptoms;
» education – debilitating conditions, learning and understanding what causes ill-health;
» caring – the increasing number of concerned employers;
» economic factors – government campaigns, sickness payments, absenteeism, putting health care problems right;
» government legislation – protecting workers, laying down basic standards, Health and Safety, labor unions;
» industry benchmarking – fast information flow, litigation, expanded knowledge and information, global concerns;
» changes in lifestyle – the increase in the number of sedentary workers, the evolution of body care to combat obesity.

"As a manager you have responsibilities to manage your activities to prevent work-related ill health. As well as protecting the health of your employees and complying with the law, good health will bring benefits to your business."

Bill Callaghan, chair, Health and Safety Commission, in the introduction to "Good Health is Good Business"

There are many factors which have influenced the evolution of body care and health care for employees. Over the years there has been no single factor which has brought about radical change in attitudes to health and body care in the workplace without there being considerable overlap with the other factors involved. In this chapter we shall consider the most important of these factors:

» litigation;
» education;
» genuine caring;
» economic factors;
» government legislation;
» industry benchmarking; and
» changes in lifestyle.

Litigation

When small boys were being sent up chimneys and miners were being sent below ground (miners still are, of course), I doubt there was a single instance of a worker taking an employer to court to seek industrial compensation for illness, injury, or ill health. Nowadays hardly a week goes by without such a case being brought and, more often than not, won. Workers, often through their labor union representatives, are increasingly aware that employers who put them at risk are liable to face legal action – and considerable awards and pay-outs are being made as the result of successful actions being pursued through the courts. A case in point is *vibrational white finger disease* (Raynaud's phenomenon), which is a disorder that affects the blood vessels in the fingers, toes, ears, and nose. Its characteristic attacks result from a constriction of these blood vessels. It is a disorder often produced by the use of high-vibration machinery such as chain saws, drills, road compacting machines and high-speed compressors. Once workers have been affected by this disease, the chances of them enjoying a full and active working life again are remote. Thus they naturally seek compensation from their employer for disability. In the UK, coal-face workers have successfully pursued claims through the courts and have been awarded compensation. In British Columbia, tree fellers have done likewise, in an industry in which approximately 50% of all chain-saw workers have reported serious symptoms.

Some of the earliest cases of court action being brought as a result of this condition date back to the 1980s in the US, where workers employed on dry-dock ship-building were reported to suffer from it as a result of using riveting machinery. Naturally, employers have sought to prove that this condition is not debilitating, and that an employee can continue to work, but perhaps in another, less arduous, capacity. Nevertheless, it is a serious condition, and it is linked to *carpal tunnel syndrome* which is one of a number of conditions in the category of repetitive strain injuries. The carpal tunnel is a flexible tube within the arm, containing a ligament that runs from the forearm through the wrist. Carpal tunnel syndrome occurs when the ligament becomes inflamed, swells up, and compresses the median nerve that runs to some of the fingers. The syndrome may cause pain in the arm and numbness and tingling in the hand and fingers. Untreated, it may lead to severely disabling muscle-weakness in the hands.

Education

Modern research is highlighting many causes of potentially debilitating conditions that previously went unchecked. Education is now a key word in body care – we all want to know how we get sick as much as how to cure the sickness. The more we learn and understand how the body works, the greater our understanding of what causes poor health. An example of this is the recent understanding that a lung condition previously considered to be smoking-related is actually *asbestosis*, and is the result of breathing in the dust of asbestos over a long period. Asbestos was developed in the 1880s as a wonder material to be used as a fireproof roofing material and a sound insulator. By 1906, the first deaths were being reported – inaccurately – as lung cancer. By 1935, the dangers of working with asbestos were well-known by the asbestos companies, but the deaths were still being attributed to lung cancer – and asbestosis went unrecognized, still thought to be a smoking-related illness. It was not until suppressed research information on the toxic properties of asbestos were "leaked" that asbestos workers became aware of the dangers and were able to demand that they be protected from the risks.

Genuine caring

Perhaps it was the hippie era of the 1960s that caused a shift in management consciousness about employee health. Previously there had been some individual managers who cared passionately about their workforce and provided decent health care – but they were a rarity. Some, such as Jesse Boot who founded the UK drugstore chain Boots, were indeed concerned. Boot took great care of the physical and social welfare of his employees. One of his innovations was organizing picnics and trips to the coast so that his employees could get a break from work. He and his wife Florence also provided cups of hot chocolate for the workers first thing in the morning, as they realized that many of their employees had had no breakfast before coming to work. Boot spent around $6 million on houses, parks and other facilities for his staff but, until the late 1960s and early 1970s, he was an exception.

During the last twenty to thirty years, there has been a considerable revolution in workers' health care that goes well beyond a desire for profitability or fear of litigation. Some managers today do genuinely care about their workforce, and seek to provide as much as is possible and practical in the way of comfort and freedom from risk.

Economic factors

The UK government started a massive public awareness campaign in 1995 entitled *Good Health is Good Business*. The aim of this campaign, which is still running, is to persuade managers that providing good health and safety procedures is not merely a legal or moral requirement but also sound financial sense. The campaign provides examples of profitable health care where the cost of implementing good practice saves money in the long term. Not only does a company save the money that it would have to spend on sickness payments, compensation, and other reparations, but it also recoups the investment through the enhancement of employee satisfaction and morale. If a company is seen to be spending money on preventative measures, then its employees are reassured that they are cared about and that their health interests are being considered. The staff are also reassured when immediate action is taken to put a health care problem right.

An example of this is a hospital where two members of the health care staff suffered serious back injuries while helping patients with severe disabilities to use the toilets. These toilets were poorly designed and it was difficult for the staff to manipulate the patients effectively. Immediate action was taken and considerable money spent redesigning the toilets, improving the lighting, and generally making them more accessible and easier to use. The risk of injury to staff and patients was reduced, and the risk of litigation was also reduced. More importantly, the staff were reassured that their health was receiving the highest priority, and morale was increased.

Spending money on health and body care is not only a wise investment but also a saving. It reduces the likelihood of:

» future litigation;
» the need for industrial compensation;
» absenteeism, with all the accompanying costs of sick pay;
» the cost of high staff turnover due to low morale; and
» being fined or worse by the courts as a result of ignoring statutory health and safety obligations. Penalties can be imposed by government agencies on employers who subject workers to unacceptably high risks.

But all this is something that has evolved. Traditionally, the workforce was regarded as a replaceable and expendable resource; what the military referred to as "cannon fodder." Nowadays, workers are seen as a vital and important asset, and are treated as such by enlightened and forward-thinking managements.

Government legislation

Over the last fifty years, governments have increasingly seen their role as protecting work forces as much as encouraging the profitability of companies. They have laid down legislation to protect workers from unscrupulous employers and have established basic standards for health and safety. This legislation covers pretty well all aspects of employment, from how many rest rooms have to be provided for any given number of employees, to sick pay and maternity benefit. Western countries have led the way but are now being followed by all the major democracies in the world. It is now standard practice for a government to regulate for the workforce of its nation so that it is protected from disease, injury, and accidents. Governments have taken on the role of prosecutors in the case of industrial accidents and have been known to send managers to court for manslaughter in severe incidents. Companies are now aware that they have to be on their guard not only against private litigation brought by injured or sick workers but also against government agencies which have been specifically set up to monitor the health of employees. Labor unions have been very instrumental in bringing this situation about, and the evolution of government regulation has run hand-in-hand with the development of increasingly sophisticated and high-powered labor unions during the twentieth century.

Industry benchmarking

Each industry has its own set of particular problems when it comes to the health of its workers. And most industries have worked in isolation in the past. What was happening to the health and safety of workers in the ship-building industry in Scotland was unknown to shipyard workers in Japan. But the arrival of computers, e-mail, and the Internet has changed this situation dramatically. When one worker is injured or suffers ill health at work, details are now quickly circulated to other workers throughout the world in the same industry. Action can be taken immediately to ensure that the same accident or injury or illness does not happen elsewhere. The same goes for the news of litigation. It took around twenty years for the first cases of asbestosis litigation in America to be repeated in the UK in the early part of the twentieth century. Today this just could not happen. There is immediate access to information so that one case that previously would have been discrete and barely noticed is now broadcast around the world to workers in a similar industry instantaneously. Health care has evolved due to high-speed communications and this evolution has expanded knowledge and information. Health care benchmarking is now a global concern and each industry expects the same procedures and standards to be prevalent everywhere in the world.

Changes in lifestyle

It was not many years ago that people walked to work, did some pretty strenuous manual laboring, dug their gardens when they got home, and generally worked longer hours and spent very little time relaxing. We have now developed into predominantly sedentary workers, and body care has evolved as a natural way to try to remedy this. We now regard as essential the gymnasiums, trimnasiums, and health clubs which have sprung up everywhere: we need them to combat the excess weight, the flabby muscles, and the lack of good healthy fresh air that our forebears would have had as part of their normal life. We spend money providing vehicles to bus our children to school, and then hold fundraisers to find even more money to provide them with fitness suites when they get there. We spend much longer indoors with air conditioning; we watch TV and sit in front of computer screens all day long, and we drive everywhere rather than walk. Health awareness and body care have grown up as a response to all these changes in our lifestyle.

The health requirements of workers have evolved to the point where we have lost sight of whose responsibility it is to maintain basic health and well-being, and since the conditions of our working environments are very much a part of this evolution, we can all with some justification expect to be protected and to have certain standards of basic care implemented by those who employ us.

Safe Working in the Office

» VDUs – safe working practices, problems caused by VDUs;
» keyboards – RSI, cumulative trauma disorder, left-handed problems, forearm pain;
» seating – adjustable chairs, right height, right position;
» lighting – glare, reflections, direct and indirect light;
» the healthy environment – checking the office, taking breaks, health and safety;
» training and feedback – what sort of training, who should do the training, who should be trained, and how;
» imaginary problems – radiation from VDUs;
» sick building syndrome – ventilation systems, building-related diseases, construction of buildings, the air we are entitled to;
» taking action – reporting symptoms.

"All too often people are made ill by their work. It is a fundamental of business to take care of your people's health and safety so that they can take care of you. Well-run businesses are invariably happy and healthy ones and profitable as well."

Sir John Harvey-Jones, UK management guru, in the introduction to the Health and Safety Commission's Good Health is Good Business

USING COMPUTERS – OUTLINING THE PROBLEMS

The computer has brought enormous benefits, but it has also brought us many physical and mental disadvantages which we did not experience in such a concentrated way before it came into our lives, at home and at work. Ever since we first sat down to look at a VDU (video display unit) and put our hands on a keyboard and a mouse we have experienced problems. In this chapter we shall examine some of the health and body care issues related to computer use.

VDUs

The VDU can cause a range of discomforts which are all unhealthy individually but can combine together to give us a potentially serious health risk. This can be insidious, the discomforts creep upon us slowly, making it difficult for us to identify them immediately as the consequences of computer use. These discomforts can include:

» headaches;
» fatigue;
» eye strain;
» neck strain;
» back pain; and
» upper limb disorders.

Because of these problems we have come to view the VDU as a source of potential risk to health.

There are several factors to consider in relation to the safe use of a VDU including:

» the flicker rate of the monitor screen;
» incorrect positioning of the VDU and the user's seat;

» reflective glare;
» badly adjusted controls, such as brightness and contrast;
» obscured vision due to dirt and dust on the screen; and
» too long a period spent at the VDU without a break.

To safeguard both yourself and any team members you may be responsible for, it is best to adopt six key points when using a VDU. These are:

1 the screen should be fitted with a swivel and tilt device;
2 the VDU should have controls to adjust brightness and contrast;
3 the top of the screen should be level with the viewer's eyes;
4 there should not be any screen flicker;
5 the VDU should be free from reflection and glare; and
6 the VDU should be kept scrupulously clean – this includes not letting people touch it with their fingers or wipe it with inappropriate materials.

The keyboard and mouse

Sorting out the VDU is only part of the battle in getting workers to enjoy good body care when it comes to using computer equipment. There is also the matter of the keyboard and the mouse. If the keyboard is badly positioned, or the mouse used in a manner that is awkward, they can subject the user's arms and hands to unnatural strain and cause repetitive strain injury (RSI). We have known for some time that repetitive movements of the arms and wrists have adverse physiological effects on the body, causing damage to nerves, muscles, and tendons. But recent research has shown that RSI is only one of a number of factors that affect our health. Research done at the University of Manchester's Unit of Chronic Disease Epidemiology by Professors Gary Macfarlane (head of the Pain Research Group) and Alan Silman in 2000 suggests that illness is a major risk factor in the onset of sudden forearm pain which lasts for more than one day.

Macfarlane and Silman suggest that terms such as *cumulative trauma disorder* and *repetitive strain injury* may be misleading as they imply a single uniform cause to the condition, and that by avoiding that single cause we might cure the condition. It would appear from their research that some form of ill health already present is a major contributory factor, as is stress. When keyboard users are stressed, they tend to press down harder on the keys or the computer mouse. In order to alert users to this potential problem, a new mouse has now been designed which squeaks when it is pressed too hard.

Left-handed workers tend to suffer from more forearm pain as most "ergonomically designed" keyboards and mice favor right-handed users. There are, however, specialized computer products which have been designed for left-handed users and these should be supplied to anyone who requires them.

The link between stress and forearm pain should be closely watched, as should the effect of other illnesses. The physical aspects of RSI can be minimized by good work practices, and we shall look at these next.

Forearm pain

Anyone who has not actually experienced the pain of RSI has no way of knowing or monitoring what is happening for the poor worker who is afflicted by it. RSI is an extremely painful condition and should be taken very seriously indeed. Taking measures to avoid anyone suffering from it in the first place is vital. We have already looked at some of the possible causes, including stress and an already present ill-health problem of another kind. But there are several ways in which we can minimize the physical factors which can bring on an attack. These include:

» not working for too long a period at any one time – taking regular breaks;
» typing gently;
» avoiding awkward movements of the hands;
» sitting comfortably – elbows level with the desk and wrists straight;
» having the chair and desk at the right height for the worker;
» keeping the feet flat on the floor when typing; and
» adopting a relaxed sitting position, and remembering to drop the neck and shoulders from time to time as stress and tension build up.

RSI is not just extremely painful, it also manifests itself as numbness or loss of movement, and in severe cases a total temporary loss of use of the hands and wrists. If it reaches that level, the worker simply cannot work. Taking painkillers is not the answer, as the pain is only one of a number of symptoms of this debilitating condition. Good effective precautions prevent the onset, and this applies to the keyboard as much as to the worker using it. Good keyboard practice includes:

» making sure the keyboard has a tilt facility;
» having a sensitive keyboard so the keys do not have to be pounded;
» updating equipment regularly so old equipment is discarded;
» having a keyboard with clear and clean symbols;
» having a document holder;
» making sure that the keyboard and screen are separate; and
» making sure there is enough space to allow the wrists to be straight when working.

Seating

Even if the keyboard, the screen, and the mouse are all ideally suited to the user, there are still factors which must be considered in terms of good body care. The chair is a vital component of the working environment. Sitting for long periods working at a computer screen can cause a wide range of conditions including:

» back ache;
» upper limb disorders including muscle strain of the arms and neck;
» upper thigh problems (the buttocks);
» eye strain; and
» headaches due to neck strain.

Having the right chair, and having it adjusted correctly, is most important. Every individual worker must monitor his or her own comfort levels, but being uncomfortable is one of the first signs of the onset of any of the problems listed above. Sitting comfort should be monitored regularly and any discomfort must be addressed immediately. The chair should fulfil five criteria for safe and comfortable working conditions:

it should have an adjustable seat height;
it should be able to be tilted;
it should have an adjustable back height;
it should be stable; and
it should be easy to use with controls that are simple and accessible.

Lighting

Solving the problems of the immediate work-station is a prerequisite to good body care, but we also have to be on guard against environmental factors outside of our immediate area. Light is one of the most important factors to get right if we are to avoid suffering from:

» headaches;
» tiredness;
» sore eyes;
» eye strain; and
» irritability.

These are all conditions brought about by poor or incorrect lighting and lighting levels. It is vital to check for potential lighting problems such as:

» direct light on the VDU user;
» reflection;
» flickering lights; and
» glare.

Direct natural light from windows, skylights, and doorways can shine on to the screen and reflect into the workers' eyes. Direct artificial light from overhead lights and desk lamps can be equally intrusive. Some equipment has lights which can flash or remain on permanently, and this can distract anyone typing if the lights are too bright or are permanently in the line of vision.

Reflected natural or artificial light – light which is not pointed directly at you – can still shine into your eyes or cause glare. Any shiny surfaces apart from the screen can cause glare and reflected light, and can cause discomfort.

It is important to check for lighting problems, especially direct light on the VDU user, glare, reflection, and flickering lights. It is also worth noting that changes in the working environment can throw up problems – changing the location of a work-station, new office furniture, new equipment, different lighting, a change in blinds or curtains can all create unforeseen hazards.

The office environment

Now that we have checked the VDU, the keyboard, the mouse, the chair, and the lighting, it is worth having a look around the whole office and making sure it is all body care conscious and safe. The following items, in brief, are worth paying attention to:

» cables and wires should be secure;
» a footrest should be provided for anyone who needs one;
» the desk surface should be non-reflective and free from glare;
» the office should be tidy, clean, and free from clutter;
» there should be a minimum of noise, and any noisy equipment should be covered if possible to reduce the noise;
» the temperature should be comfortable and adjustable;
» the humidity should be comfortable and adjustable; and
» the windows should have adjustable curtains or blinds to shut out glare or excess light.

These factors are important and should be attended to, to make each and every individual employee's work safe and healthy.

Earlier we looked at taking breaks from work, and the importance of taking regular breaks cannot be over-stressed to avoid problems with RSI, fatigue, headaches, and back pain. But it is worth noting that breaks should be taken *away from* the desk or work-station. All too often we stop for a breather or cup of coffee and stay rooted to the chair. We need to:

» get away from the VDU, even if we are not looking directly at it;
» get up and walk about for exercise;
» get some fresh air from time to time;
» socialize a little and interact with our colleagues – if we work alone or from home we should consider having a pet to talk to (it really does help); and
» go and sit somewhere else for a while – this eases the strain on muscles and stops us getting too complacent about our sitting position,

Taking a break can mean an opportunity to do other work tasks, such as photocopying, filing, and collecting or delivering documents to other parts of the building. The important thing is to give our hands and eyes a rest as these are the things most used – do not take a break and then spend it reading or writing in longhand, a break should be a hand and eye break, and not just a temporary shift in routine.

If we do notice we are suffering any form of RSI, back ache, persistent headaches, or eye strain we should immediately:

» report it to a Health and Safety Officer;
» report it to a union official;
» report it to our immediate supervisor/manager; and
» report it to our general practitioner.

We should also check everything that has been previously mentioned with regard to VDUs, keyboards, chairs, and lighting in order to identify causes and reasons for the discomfort or pain.

Training and feedback

We all assume that we know how to use a keyboard and VDU. But do we? Computer work is usually something that we get trained in, but it is less likely that the training has included the ergonomics of using the equipment: there is always a correct way and many incorrect ways, and it is vital to good body care that users recognize this.

The only effective training in good computer use is one-to-one tuition with a qualified trainer. If that is not possible, here are a few guidelines as to what we should be looking at with regard to training:

» our rights and procedures – we need to know who to go to and what we should do if we have physical body care problems;
» when, and how, to take breaks and what benefit they have;
» how to adjust the chair;
» how to use the keyboard properly;
» how to sit in relation to the screen and keyboard;
» how to recognize potential problems and what to do to resolve them;
» how to recognize hazards such as faulty plug sockets, damaged electrical wiring, and dangerous equipment, and what to do about them;
» procedures for reporting problems that we cannot deal with ourselves; and

» what sort of lighting requirements we need, and how to adjust lighting correctly to avoid glare, reflection, or poor quality lights.

Unfounded problems

Some people worry about the effects of radiation from a VDU. *There is no evidence whatsoever* that radiation from a VDU is a hazard. But any amount of reassurance might not stop some people worrying about it. If you work with someone who has a genuine worry (or if you worry about it yourself) it is worth:

» being sympathetic – do not dismiss concerns about health or safety out of hand; we all have private fears and radiation is an understandable if unfounded worry;
» present the facts – there is no evidence to prove VDUs are harmful and the UK's National Radiological Protection Board has stated that the levels of radiation from a computer monitor are well below what could be considered to be hazardous;
» make sure they have had proper training – with appropriate training they feel reassured and comforted; and
» make sure the worry does not conceal genuine problems such as RSI or eye strain – it is easy to focus so much on an imaginary problem that the real ones are overlooked and physical symptoms are attributed to the wrong cause.

MOBILE PHONES

There is increasing evidence that mobile phones do have a detrimental effect on health and they should be used with some caution. Their use should be limited and they should not be pressed to the ear for long periods: a remote listening device should be used instead. Habitual users of mobile phones – particularly children and young adults – are often unaware of the potential damage they may be doing to themselves, just as they are oblivious to the intense annoyance they can cause to others by using a mobile phone in a public place.

SICK BUILDING SYNDROME

Throughout this chapter we have looked at our immediate working environment, but it is also worth taking a quick look at a new syndrome

that has become newsworthy over the past few years – sick building
syndrome, or SBS.

We spend a considerable amount of time at work and we do suffer
ill effects from it at times. Experts have recently noticed that the actual
building in which we work may be responsible for such ill health. They
have found that ill health caused by sick buildings can be divided into
two distinct types:

» Building-related diseases – illnesses brought about within a building,
  such as colds and other infections which can spread through an
  office, allergies and asthma brought on by dust or mould, or even
  cancer triggered by asbestos, or pesticides, or harmful chemicals
  stored in the building.
» Sick buildings – illnesses brought about from the actual construction
  of a building, such as the case in 1976 of 182 mysterious cases
  of serious pneumonia which afflicted members of the American
  Legion attending a conference in Philadelphia. This was not normal
  pneumonia but a new bacterial organism – named *Legionella pneu-
  mophila* – which develops in the warm water of a building's cooling
  tower. When water vapor mists from that water are transferred into
  the building through the ventilation system, mass illness can occur.
  Other sources of ill health can be traced to humidifiers contami-
  nated with microbes that can trigger asthma and hypersensitivity
  pneumonitis. Other toxins may be conducted into the building by
  the air-duct system; these can include fibrous glass which causes
  mysterious itching. Improperly used carpet-cleaning fluids can be
  conducted around the building through air ducts, causing coughing
  and throat irritation. These conditions, by their very nature, can be
  difficult to identify, difficult to prove, and difficult to rectify.

Anyone complaining of unexplained illness should be on the lookout for the condition being brought on by the actual building itself.
Modern buildings contain a staggering array of chemicals, plastics, toxic
materials, and fumes from paint, office supplies, and photocopiers. The
amount of air we are "entitled" to at work has also been drastically
reduced to around five cubic feet of outdoor air per person per minute.
This may well have lowered the ventilation standards below what might
be considered healthy.

It would appear from research carried out by the Division of Allergy and Immunology at the University of South Florida that some people become so sick from their work building that they are unable to go to work at all. It has been found that work stress can trigger symptoms in people who otherwise may not have fallen prey to any condition – a weakened system is more likely to respond badly to toxins than one which is working effectively and healthily.

Alan Hedge, associate professor of design and environmental analysis at Cornell University, has been studying SBS for over ten years. Although his researches have found no correlation between sick buildings and tobacco smoke, carbon monoxide, carbon dioxide, formaldehyde, temperature or humidity, the idea of studying mineral fibres came from a woman worker in one of the buildings under study. She kept a small air filter on her desk and asked Hedge to study what it trapped. Hedge traced the fibres he found to the ceiling tiles over her head.

Taking action

Whether the problem is stress or bad air or poor lighting (fluorescent lights have been found to trigger headaches in a large number of workers), workers who ignore their symptoms are not helping the problem. Problems must be reported and examinations of the buildings carried out so that the source of the problem can be identified and action taken to put things right.

The Balance between Home and Work

» The one-in-ten factor – 10% of workers claim the work/home relationship is out of balance;
» five major work-related problem areas – demands of the job, job changes, interpersonal relationships, management practices, job control;
» six major home-related problem areas – finances, general demands, relationships, living arrangements, illness/death, children;
» phoning in sick – absenteeism and poor health care;
» the snowball effect – not maintaining a good health and body care regime exacerbates any problems;
» ignoring the warnings – what employers should be doing to encourage good practice;
» how healthy are we? – a questionnaire to determine your own ill-health warning signals;
» keeping fit and taking regular exercise – the key to improving the work/home balance;
» types of exercise that are not boring.

Take a tea break

Modern research has shown that drinking four or five cups of tea a day can reduce the incidence of heart disease by 44%. It can also diminish the risk of developing pancreatic, prostate, stomach, and lung cancer. And since drinking a lot of tea increases fluid intake, it helps to stave off conditions such as constipation and cystitis. Tea's medical benefits are attributed to the presence of antioxidants called flavanoids - one cup of tea is so full of flavanoids that it can do more to fight heart disease and cancer than regular intakes of fruit and vegetables. Other nutrients in tea include potassium, which helps maintain a healthy heartbeat, and manganese, which is essential for bone growth. So taking an extra tea break or two may be extremely beneficial.

GOING HOME

No matter how dedicated we are and how hard we work, there comes a time when we have to go home. And no matter how much we love being at home there comes a time when we need to go to work. We cannot escape either and it is very hard to separate the two when it comes to matters of health and body care. What we do at work affects our home life and the opposite is obviously true.

On average we spend some ten and a half hours a day (working day that is) actually at work or travelling to get there. We then spend about four hours doing household chores, having time with our children and eating, washing, that sort of stuff. Once we add in time for sleeping, there is not a lot of time left. So what time are we dedicating to ourselves? Very little. We have so little personal time that it is hard to eliminate the effects of stress we build up or to dedicate a little time to ourselves for exercise, thinking about our health or diet, working out a health care program, or even having a quiet sit down with our feet up.

One in ten

Most of us are able to carry on like this for quite a long time, but one in ten of us does report experiencing excess worry, nerves, or stress because we have trouble balancing the home/work relationship. That percentage represents a lot of working people. Can we find out more about these one in ten? Well, yes. It would appear that women are almost twice as likely as men to experience difficulties – around 17% of women. And the younger we are the less we are likely to have problems – that is until we hit 30 when the trouble begins. Between 30 and 45 are the most troublesome ages for men – that is when we are most likely to be bringing up a family and building a career simultaneously.

The more education we have, the harder we find it to juggle the home/work balance. That seems to be because more highly educated people are in more professional jobs, which means they are expected to work harder and longer, thus making it more difficult for them.

So which bit is causing the problems? Is it the stress of bringing up children and running a home that is affecting our work? Or is it the stress of work that is affecting our home life? It would appear to be a pretty even split. Around 50% of the one in ten report that having it easier at home would make it easier at work, while the other 50% report that having it easier at work would make it easier at home. This is not a book about home relationships, but it is clear that what we can put into practice at work may help at home as well.

The five major work-related problem areas

There seem to be five major problem areas that affect workers so much that it spills over into their home life:

» the demands of the job itself – too much work, too stressful, too tiring;
» job changes – changes in personnel, routine and procedures, and tasks;
» interpersonal relationships – not getting on with colleagues;
» management practices – poor management, bullying management; and
» job control – lack of feedback, poor communication, lack of input.

These seem to be pretty evenly spread, with job demands being the highest category of dissatisfaction and around 50% of workers claiming that trouble with job demands affects their home life.

The six major home-related problem areas

At home the major problem factors appear to be:

- » problems with finances;
- » general demands;
- » relationship difficulties;
- » living arrangements;
- » illness or death in the family; and
- » children.

It seems that the worst of these is relationship problems, with around 35% of us reporting that they affect our work.

The worst health and body care records

If we then go on to examine the health of those who report that the work/home relationship is breaking down, we find that the majority of the one in ten are those with the worst health care and body care records. Of those one in ten, over 40% take no regular physical activities for health or exercise, 24% smoke, and 20% use alcohol to excess.

Could it be that the healthier we are the less we are likely to experience problems with the work/home relationship? It would certainly seem so. Those of us who are active, health conscious, and maintain a nutritional and well-balanced diet are much less likely to suffer problems with balancing work and home.

Phoning in sick

So what happens when the relationship between home and work breaks down? We report in sick. Almost one in five of us will miss one week of work per year as a result of sickness. And one third of those of us who report in sick will stay away from work for five weeks a year or longer – that's around 6% of the total work force. That is a lot of people phoning in sick for a lot of time. And it is a lot of work time lost too.

Even the healthy ones amongst us will report in sick at some time – around two thirds of us will miss the odd day here and there. 25% of us will miss around two days a year and over 20% of us will miss between three and five days. Absenteeism is higher amongst women than men – 78% compared to 63%.

Absenteeism is directly related to the work/home relationship. Employees free from home stress are much less likely to phone in sick than those who are experiencing problems with relationships or children, illness in the family or financial problems.

The snowball effect

Earlier we looked at how those of us who try to stay healthy suffer less from the home/work relationship problem. Well, the same seems to be true of absenteeism as well. Those of us who take regular exercise, eat healthily, avoid alcohol to excess, and do not smoke are far less likely to phone in sick than those who ignore those issues. The less attention we pay to these issues the longer we stay off work. The greater the number of unfavorable health practices, the greater the likelihood that we will report in sick. This is why it makes economic sense to encourage good body and health care practices in employees. If we do not, a snowball effect develops – it just keeps getting worse.

So to recap, if we take exercise on a regular basis, eat healthily, stop smoking, and avoid alcohol to excess we:

» are less likely to experience work/home relationship problems – we seem better able to get the balance right;
» experience fewer problems at work itself – we are better able to cope with the problems work throws at us;
» experience fewer problems at home – we cope better with children, relationships and the general stresses that home can generate; and
» report in sick less often – and take less time off.

Ignoring warnings

So what are we waiting for? Well, it would seem that no matter how many facts and statistics we present to workers, there will always be around one in ten of us that choose to ignore such warnings. The individual employee will often prefer to select his or her own health care program – or lack of one. Concerted effort must be made – on a financial basis alone to decrease absenteeism – to encourage good health care practices amongst employees. We have to:

» provide the resources and facilities, at work, for good body care such as ergonomically designed work-stations;

» reduce stress factors at work by giving workers more control, more say in their environment, and by improving management techniques to make workers feel more involved and more responsible;

» take a proactive approach to safety training, implementing physical exercise programs, and encouraging flexitime so that workers can arrange their own work/home balance better;

» provide detailed feedback to employees about the relationship between good body care management and absenteeism;

» be more understanding of workers who are experiencing problems at home, and provide more support, care, counseling, back up, and even financial assistance if needed;

» provide more information about diet, healthy exercise, and the problems with smoking and excess usage of alcohol; and

» encourage good body care practices – by setting a good example ourselves we are more likely to encourage workers than if we scoff at ideas of getting and staying healthy.

How healthy are we?

The healthier we are, the less likely we are to get sick or experience work/home relationship problems. So how healthy are we? Only we can judge that, but do we stop to consider it? Do we ever take a little of that rare and precious time we mentioned earlier to check that we are healthy? It is important every now and again just to run a quick check to make sure we are as healthy as we ought to be. Take a couple of minutes to complete the simple questionnaire in Table 5.1 to see how good your health and body care regime is at the moment. Bear in mind that some questions relate to your emotional health, but this can affect your physical health to a large degree.

Answer the questions as honestly as you can and give yourself the following points:

Never: 0
Rarely: 1
Occasionally: 2
Often: 3
Always: 4

Table 5.1

Tick boxes and add up your score at the end

I am irritable	☐
I am lethargic	☐
I am physically run down	☐
I am pressurized all the time	☐
I am short of breath	☐
I am tense and nervous generally	☐
I am worried I might have a breakdown	☐
I cry easily and feel emotional	☐
I drink too much	☐
I eat irregularly	☐
I feel dizzy, faint, or far away	☐
I feel exhausted	☐
I feel tension in my neck, shoulders, and chest	☐
I get a lot of headaches and migraines	☐
I have constant niggling pains	☐
I have difficulty concentrating	☐
I have high blood pressure (if you don't know your blood pressure mark it as a 4)	☐
I have high cholesterol (if you don't know your cholesterol level mark it as a 4)	☐
I have no interest in sex	☐
I have palpitations and panic attacks	☐
I have sexual problems	☐
I have trouble relaxing	☐
I have trouble sleeping	☐
I smoke	☐
I suffer from asthma	☐
I suffer from constant infections/colds etc	☐
I suffer from fluid retention	☐
I suffer from upset stomachs and have poor bowel movement	☐
I suffer recurring digestion problems	☐
I take drugs/medication to help me get through the day	☐
Final total	☐

When you have answered each of these questions and given yourself the appropriate points you can add them up and score your own ill health warning signal level.

» Under 20 points - you seem to be showing no signs of ill health. No action needed.
» 20-30 - Mild ill-health signals. You need to look at what this is and rectify it.
» 30-40 - Moderate ill-health signals. This could be beginning to affect your long-term health and you had better pay some serious attention to what is causing it.
» 40-60 - Above average ill-health signals - you need both to look at what is causing it and to do something about it, as well as having a health check-up, and monitoring your long-term health plans.
» 60-80 - High ill-health signals. There is something wrong with your lifestyle and you need to do something about it immediately. The ill health you are encountering is simply too high.
» More than 80 points - Very high ill-health signals. If you do not take prompt and effective action you may be at risk of serious illness. Do something about it now.

Once you have had a think about your own emotional and physical health, you can decide what to do about it - see Chapter 7 for information on implementing a personal body and health care program.

Regular exercise is the key

It is worth bearing in mind that regular exercise does seem to be the key to quite a lot of health care issues. Keeping physically fit is important. Doing some form of exercise improves body function as well as aiding relaxation, improving our sex life, enhancing our overall well-being, and increasing our "happiness quota."

Keeping fit will improve both our work/home relationship and reduce the number of days off we take. It has the following effects:

» it builds up confidence;
» it causes the body to release *endorphins* (hormones) which act as natural anti-depressants;
» it eases muscular tension, increases energy levels, and strengthens all the muscles of the body;
» it enables the heart rate to return to normal more quickly after any strenuous exertion, improves the efficiency of the heart, lowers the heart rate generally, and protects you from heart disease;

» it makes you more resistant to infections, and enables you to recover more quickly from illness;
» it improves breathing and lung function;
» it improves and maintains good circulation, lowers blood pressure, and reduces both fat and cholesterol in the bloodstream;
» it improves suppleness, strength, stamina, and self-image;
» it improves the body's immune system;
» it reduces stress levels; and
» it increases longevity.

It doesn't have to be boring

That is not a bad list of benefits for a little regular exercise. But what are you actually going to do? Many people are put off exercise because they think that it is boring or too routine, and that they will not be able to stick to it. There are, however, many things you can do which you might not think of as exercise but which do the job effectively – and in a fun and entertaining way. Some of these could never be considered boring:

» badminton – good all-round fitness;
» canoeing – good all-round fitness;
» cycling – good for stamina and strength;
» dancing – good all-round fitness;
» football – good all-round fitness;
» golf – good all-round fitness;
» gymnastics – good all-round fitness;
» jogging – good for stamina;
» martial arts – good for suppleness;
» rock climbing – good for stamina and strength;
» rowing – improves stamina and strength;
» squash – good all-round fitness;
» swimming – excellent for good all-round fitness;
» tennis – good all-round fitness;
» walking – good all-round fitness;
» weightlifting – improves strength; and
» yoga – good for improving suppleness.

Some of these can be taken up with a partner, with children, or with friends, which can help considerably with the work/home/social relationship.

The State of the Art in Body Care

» Work-related illnesses – breathing problems, exposure to biological agents, exposure to radiation, heavy lifting, high noise levels, poor work postures, stress, vibration;
» recognizing the hazards – talking to staff, monitoring sickness levels, checking materials, walking around;
» preparing a risk assessment document – steps to be taken to minimize hazards, setting targets, staff training;
» economic, moral, and legal obligations;
» checking for problems;
» increased heart disease factor in night shift workers;
» exhaustion and commuter stress;
» dealing with stress;
» implementing a sound health and body care policy;
» listening to complaints and the suggestion box;
» the follow-up – motivating staff to enhance their body care.

Regular jogging cannot help prevent men putting on weight in middle age, according to Dr Paul Williams of the Lawrence Berkeley National Laboratory in California. He has studied 7000 male joggers and discovered that they put on just as much weight between the ages of 18 and 50 as men who have never jogged, with the average male gaining 3.3lb for every decade of life. "The perception is that people gain weight as they get older due to inactivity," Dr Williams said. "Our study suggests this does not seem to be the case." He said there were physiological reasons why men put on weight as they got older, with the decline in testosterone levels being a significant factor.

In Britain around two million people suffer from ill health caused by work, and around 18 million working days are lost each year as people take time off work because work has made them ill. This lost working time costs around 11 billion pounds. Work-related illness is a major cause of absenteeism and problems with the work/home balance – which we looked at in Chapter 5. No matter what size the business, protecting workers from ill health caused by their work is of vital importance.

Businesses which have implemented good health care schemes report that absenteeism drops and the general morale and well-being of their work force increases. But what is good practice? That is what this chapter is all about: what the conscientious manager can do to make sure that team members stay fit and healthy, motivated, and physically active.

WORK-RELATED ILLNESS

First we have to be certain that we know what a work-related illness is. There are some people who are employed who will get sick – they will contract a major illness or disease which is nothing to do with their employment – no matter what job they do. These people do not come into the work-related illness category. A work-related illness is one which is specifically caused by an employment. If you did not do the job, you would not get the illness or injury or condition.

So what are we looking at here? These are the sorts of illnesses, injuries or conditions that work may be causing our employees:

» breathing – breathing in dangerous substances such as asbestos, solvents or dust, causing asthma, bronchitis, or even cancer;
» exposure to biological agents – viruses, bacteria and fungi, general sickness, hepatitis, legionnaires' disease;
» exposure to radiation – burns, skin disorders, cancer, eye damage;
» heavy lifting – musculoskeletal disorders, sprains and strains, back pain or injury;
» high noise levels – tinnitus, deafness;
» poor work postures – RSI, upper limb disorders, back pain;
» stress – high blood pressure, heart disease, depression, mental illness; and
» vibration – vibrational white finger disease, lower back pain, pain in fingers and joints, loss of grip.

The work place can be hazardous. It is up to us, as managers, to maintain a constant vigil against poor work practice and slipping standards, as well as implementing good health care practice in the first place.

Good health and body care management is about identifying and controlling the risks before they cause illness or injury.

Do you have a problem?

Well, do you? How do you know? If you have not looked lately you cannot possibly know. If you have not looked lately you have two potential problems – work risks *and* poor management. The effective manager should be:

» Talking to staff – to find out their views, what they think, what they regard as potential hazards, what is affecting their health and physical well-being; to listen to their complaints – no matter how trivial – because they may be clues to major problems that have gone unnoticed.
» Checking records of sickness – you need to know what sort of illnesses are affecting your staff – the frequency and the length of illness. Your sickness records may give you some very valuable clues about what is making your staff ill.

» Making sure that the hazards of any materials your staff – and you of course – handle are known about, including mundane items you may overlook such as photocopier toner, cleaning fluids, inks, and the like. Check with the suppliers of anything toxic that you use that you have up-to-date information sheets and booklets. Make this information available: ensure all the staff have copies, or that they are posted up where everyone can see them clearly, and that they have signed that they have read – and understood – them.

» Taking a regular walk round and checking every aspect of your working environment for potential health hazards – see Chapter 4 for safe working practices for work-stations. Watch how your staff work. Look at what they are doing and how they are doing it for clues as to what could affect them adversely.

Once you have appraised all the potential health and body care issues your staff can face, you will have to decide what action to take. You need to prepare a risk assessment document of some sort. If you do not have the authority to make changes yourself, you will need to present this document to someone who can authorize and implement the changes that might be necessary to safeguard your staff.

In this document you should:

» point out the potential dangers;
» include any sickness statistics to back up your argument;
» identify the steps that need to be taken to minimize the risk;
» prioritize the risks so you have a plan for implementation – it is often impossible to do everything immediately;
» set targets for reducing the health hazards;
» set control measures for making sure all plant and equipment is working correctly and is serviced and maintained at the proper intervals;
» list all protective equipment and clothing that is missing or not being used properly; and
» list what training the staff should have, and how often it should be given.

When you have done this you cannot sit back and rest. Implementing health and body care safety is an ongoing process. You cannot afford to drop your guard. Employees are well known for taking short cuts, ignoring safety warnings, forgetting their training, deliberately choosing to take risks, and often being plain downright lazy about good health and safety. You have to be their eyes and ears, their conscience, their guardian, and their protector. And at the same time you must never let them know. They have to be given responsibility for their own health and body care. They have to be allowed to work freely without feeling that their manager is fussing over them, but at the same time you must maintain your vigilance.

Why are we doing this?

Easy. To save money. Money spent on sickness payments would be better spent on preventative measures or reinvested in the company. And it is not just sickness payments, it is also the cost of high staff turnover – too many sicknesses affect morale detrimentally and people just move on – and your insurance company will raise premiums or choose not to cover you at all if there are too many claims. Health risks at work affect staff; employees work badly if they feel that they are at risk, they are not motivated if the management is not seen to be doing everything possible to improve things. Even a minor complaint that is not listened to, and action taken to rectify it, can lead to a decrease in productivity. Staff take their health seriously and so should you.

Never forget you have legal obligations to protect your staff and you run the risk of prosecution if you fail them. And you also have a moral obligation to do so.

What are we checking for?

When we do our walk round the workplace, what exactly is it we are looking for? What should we be guarding against? Table 6.1 shows a list of potential hazards and their repercussions.

Staying abreast of current research

Of course there is a wide range of factors which can affect the health of your workers that you may be entirely unaware of. The good manager tries to stay abreast of all new research and information as it surfaces. An example of this is the risk that night workers face of increased heart

Table 6.1

Hazard	What to look for	The risks
Excessive noise	Any worker who has to shout to be heard: anyone having difficulty being heard by anyone within 6 feet of them.	Excessive noise from machinery can damage hearing permanently. Once a worker's hearing has been damaged by noise there is no cure – it is permanent. Noise can also cause tinnitus, stress, sleep problems and reduced efficiency.
Breathing problems	Look for dusty conditions, broken or faulty air conditioning, ventilation systems, and closed environments where fresh air cannot circulate freely. Look for any danger of fumes from toxic substances being inadvertently breathed in, such as from photocopier toner.	Breathing in noxious fumes or toxins can cause asthma, wheezing, chest tightness, rhinitis (runny or stuffy nose), permanent lung damage, cancer (see below), and allergic reactions. Be on the lookout for headaches, nausea, dizziness and impaired co-ordination. In severe cases, unconsciousness and even death are attributable to work-related breathing problems.

(continued)

Table 6.1 *(continued)*.

Hazard	What to look for	The risks
Musculoskeletal disorders	Look for poor working conditions, highly repetitive physical work, manual handling of large, awkward or heavy objects. Excessive bending, stretching, pushing, or pulling as part of a worker's duties.	Musculoskeletal disorders can manifest themselves in a variety of ways including back pain, RSI, loss of strength in the arms, swelling or tingling in the wrists, slipped discs, upper limb disorders, pain or swelling in the hands, muscular aches and pains, strains, and sprains.
Cancer	Look for any worker handling dangerous chemicals.	Diagnosis is beyond the scope of this book. See your government's Code of Practice for handling carcinogens.
Skin disorders	Look for workers handling substances which are known to cause adverse reactions with their bare hands. Make sure protective gloves are worn when necessary. Make sure all employees have decent hand-washing facilities.	Look for skin redness, scaling, itching, excessive dryness, blistering and bleeding. Dermatitis can be serious and can spread over the entire body if treatment is not undertaken in time.

(continued)

Table 6.1 *(continued).*

Hazard	What to look for	The risks
Vibrational disorders	Be on the lookout for any workers using machinery which vibrates, including drills, chain saws, tools, and machinery.	Be on the lookout for painful fingers, tingling in the hands and wrists, loss of manual dexterity and finger blanching. Early warning symptoms are any loss of sensation in the nerves, muscles, bones, or joints in the hands, wrists, or arms.

disease. Working at night would not normally attract the attention of a conscientious manager who is looking for health and body care risks. But the link has now been made. New research has shown that the constant switching of sleeping patterns and changes in routine that night shift workers have to endure places a significant risk on the heart with the increased likelihood of heart disease. Research conducted by the University of Milan showed that the body's regular 24-hour pattern of hormone release and nerve impulses was no different in night workers than in regular workers. What this means is that hormones such as *cortiol*, which is released during the day to help the body stay awake, is missing at night, leaving the night worker without the protection and therefore more vulnerable. The body is designed to be awake during the day and to sleep at night. All its systems are geared to work with such a routine, and night workers are forcing their bodies to work under unnatural conditions, with potential dangerous consequences for their health.

Night workers also face changes in their actual working conditions. There is not the social environment for them that day workers have. Food facilities may be severely curtailed, with canteens closed, and workers at night having no choice but to bring in their own food.

Night workers also have to sleep during the day, with all the resulting problems of too much light, noise, family demands, and interruptions.

Being on the lookout for the increased risk of heart disease in night workers may be something we had not thought of - and of course we would not think of it. We are managers, not medical people or university researchers. But, as managers, what we *can* do is manage information. This is what we are best at, and managing information means monitoring health websites, reading the latest health pages in newspapers, and making sure we have all the government's latest leaflets and guidance booklets.

We also have to be on the lookout for our staff showing signs of poor body care in unlikely and entirely unexpected ways. For instance, a recent survey showed that doctors reported a 50% increase in the number of workers in the 25–35 age group who claim to suffer from exhaustion. Chronic exhaustion is not something we might expect from white collar workers. We usually associate it with people doing heavy physical work rather than those using keyboards and computers. Working conditions do seem to be a major contributory factor in this recent phenomenon. Around half of all workers in offices claim to feel exhausted after a day's toil. Fluorescent lights, poor air conditioning, and lack of natural stimulation all contribute to this. The cure seems to be a revised style of working conditions, with better lighting and better fresh air facilities. Workers also need to watch their diet and to take regular exercise. They need to avoid smoking and to watch their alcohol intake. More sleep and taking time off are also recommended. Eating properly and sleeping properly - sound advice.

Commuting stress

Some workers are becoming unhealthy on their way to work. Before they even get to the office door they have already accumulated more than their fair share of stress and poor body care. Obviously managers cannot do anything about uncomfortable and badly designed car and train seats, nor can they do anything about commuter stress caused by delays and long journeys. But they can help the poor worker who has struggled in despite the odds. Commuters should be given the chance to recover before being deluged under the next mountain of work.

In the UK, it is estimated that nearly seven million working days are lost each year through people taking time off due to stress. And this stress is costing UK businesses nearly four billion pounds a year. Extrapolate this out across the US, Europe, and Asia and the cost is vast, staggering, unbelievable. The subject of stress is covered in detail by another book in the ExpressExec series, but the good manager has to know that stress can manifest itself as physical symptoms – body care and stress management have to run hand in hand. You do need to know the top tips for dealing with stress in your workers:

» do not allow an ill worker to continue working – send him or her home to recover;
» make sure there is someone for a stressed worker to talk to – a counsellor, fellow worker, union representative, therapist, sympathetic colleague;
» get them to use some physical activity to work the stress off;
» encourage them to avoid smoking, excess alcohol, and caffeine;
» get them to take proper rest breaks and periods away from the work-station;
» make sure they fully understand personal time management – read Ros Jay's *Time Management* in the ExpressExec series; it is simply brilliant at teaching people to organize their time better and more effectively;
» try to facilitate a calm and stress-free working environment where people co-operate and work pleasantly towards a common goal;
» encourage workers to relax and make sure they are taught relaxation techniques that they can use at work;
» make sure the rest area is indeed restful and not a converted broom cupboard. It really should be a purpose-designed restful area;
» encourage them to see stressful situations as a challenge rather than a negative experience. Encourage them to grow and to relish change and new experiences; and
» encourage an environment where health, stress, and good body care are easy subjects to broach and not treated as laughable or taboo.

Working with what we have got

This chapter is about good working practices for maintaining and implementing a good body care program, so it makes sense to look at the wider picture. Work your workers to death and they will have to be replaced. Replacing workers is expensive – advertising, interviewing, training – and time consuming. It is better to work with what you have got, and to make the very best use of them. Treat them badly and they will get sick, leave, work poorly, and be disruptive – and all of these will cost your company money. Look after them and they will stay, be healthy, work harder and better, and be co-operative and helpful. Well looked-after staff are an asset. Poorly looked-after staff are a liability. Looking after your workers' health and body care is not some namby-pamby, liberal, New Age philosophy, or a new-fangled business fad. It is pure economics – build health, save money.

One of the biggest threats to workers' health is excessive working hours. It makes no economic sense to work people too long or too hard. Their productivity will fall and their morale and motivation will plummet accordingly. Even so, research has shown that 80% of workplaces have employees who work more than their standard hours, and nearly 40% of these work for no extra pay. Nearly 20% of workers are unaware of their rights regarding maternity and paternity leave, sickness entitlement, illness or injury compensation, or even their basic rights regarding good health and safety practices. So as a good manager you must ensure the following:

» that all workers know their rights and entitlements;
» that they are paid for any work they do in excess of their normal working hours;
» that their normal working hours are adhered to as far as possible – hire in more people to cover higher workloads, rather than damaging the workers you have already got;
» that they are encouraged to use flexitime – workers like it and it motivates them;
» that part-time work is available for those who want it – they like it and it motivates them;
» that basic facilities such as a crèche are available for those who need them;
» that you are open to suggestions about good working practices;
» that you listen to complaints, no matter how trivial – the first death from asbestos-related illness was someone who probably complained at some time of a tickly cough; and
» that you are nice to the staff yourself.

Nasty bosses cause sick people

The last item in the list above is not there for fun. It is a fact – nasty bosses cause more absenteeism than pretty well anything else. New research has revealed the interesting fact that workers who are scared of their bosses are twice as likely to take days off than genuinely sick ones. And workers in companies who are downsizing are less likely to do so – they are scared of losing their job. So fear is a pretty motivating force. And no, you cannot try to scare them by threatening to downsize. The research shows that workers who are frightened of downsizing and do not take days off for illness are actually less productive and are in danger of serious long-term health problems.

So be nice to them, give them plenty of breaks and make sure they get their tea.

Listening to suggestions

We looked earlier at listening to complaints no matter how trivial they seemed at the time. Workers are, however, often reluctant to complain for fear that they may be ridiculed or singled out for punishment. But you still want to hear their views, their suggestions, and their complaints. The answer might be to put up a health and safety suggestion box. This way they can tell you what is wrong in private, even anonymously, and safe in the knowledge that they will not be seen to be the whistle-blower or the office sneak. To ensure that it is effective, a suggestion box must be:

» treated seriously: anything in it must be acted upon;
» easily seen and accessible, but not so public that people putting papers in can be monitored by their colleagues;
» first installed when the maximum number of staff will be present – i.e. not during the holidays or last thing in the evening;
» open to any suggestions and not necessarily ones about their own health or safety – you are looking for suggestions about good working practices in the workplace, personal resources, rest periods, breaks, anything related to the comfort of your staff;
» followed up immediately – let your staff know what suggestions have been received and what you are doing about them; and
» properly explained when it is installed – talk to the staff about it and answer all their queries about why it is there.

Follow up

Do not sit back and think that you have finished yet. There are still a few things to do to augment good working practice. For a start, you should be raising your workers' awareness of health issues. We have already looked at how you can develop your safety and health procedures at work, but how about inviting someone in who could give a demonstration on something useful such as massage, or aromatherapy, or the Alexander Technique? Why not get a physiotherapist to come in and show the staff how to reduce back pain or muscle strain? You could post a list of community services that are specifically designed to help body care issues. You could offer stress-busting seminars and workshops. You can encourage your team members to bring in newsworthy items and pin them on a central bulletin board for the benefit of others. You could host a theme day and tie it in with a national campaign, such as Heart Month (February), Nutrition Month (March), or Cancer Month (April).

You could award a prize to the member of staff who comes up with the most innovative way of encouraging exercise, such as parking one block further away each day and walking in to work, or prizes for the most nutritional and tasty lunch menu idea. Start a no-smoking campaign that is fun – everyone has to dress up as their favourite brand – or how about a drive to reduce alcohol consumption, with everyone bringing in recipes for mouth-watering soft drinks? Sponsor your staff in a five-a-side football or softball competition – challenge other departments. Get a martial arts exponent to come in and give a demonstration, or encourage the staff to find out about T'ai Chi – see Chapter 8 for further information.

In the staff rest area, make sure there is plenty of choice of drinks and snacks – not just coffee and tea but herbal teas, nutritional soft drinks, mineral water, fresh fruit, healthy snacks, and lots of information on nutrition and good eating habits.

Brighten up the place with plants and fresh flowers – it makes economic sense, remember, to inspire and motivate your staff. Healthy staff last longer, work better, take less time off – and all for the price of a bunch of daffodils.

On warm and sunny days encourage the staff to go outside and get fresh air on their breaks, rather than sitting indoors. Encourage them to get up from their work-station and walk around a lot - walking people are creative people, they come up with better ideas when they are thinking on their feet.

Sound economic sense

Good management practice is sound economic sense - and it gets you fit as well. Remember to take an active part in any activities you set up for your staff. Seeing you involved is much more likely to get them motivated. The more encouraging and inspiring you are the more they will participate. The more remote you are the more likely they are to do likewise - they will take their lead from you. You need to be committed, involved, determined, motivating, inspiring, leading, innovative, reassuring, and healthy - and then they too will be so.

Body Care in Practice

» Work stress – home and work, job satisfaction, position, responsibility, working pressure, work relationships;
» eliminating stress from work – being assertive, being clear, being comfortable, being committed, being focused, being healthy, being organized, being safe, delegating, eating sensibly, having a fixed working day, having a life, having goals, taking breaks, working to live, support;
» top twenty tips for freeing up mental attitudes and mental approach;
» hobbies;
» an action plan;
» physical activities – gardening, walking, bicycling;
» housework;
» case study – Robert Paterson – www.warriors.org.uk

Drinking coffee has already been shown to raise anxiety levels and blood pressure, but it may also make you lose your temper, says Marc Parmentier of the Institute for Interdisciplinary Research in Brussels. Caffeine, he explains, blocks a ''receptor'' chemical in the brain that induces a calming effect on our minds. Male mice genetically engineered to simulate the effects of regular coffee drinking were found to be unusually aggressive.

RECOGNIZING STRESS AND ITS EFFECTS

One of the major contributing factors to ill health caused by work is stress. This is not a book about stress, but it is important to realize that stress manifests itself as many physical symptoms. Stress is not just an emotional or mental condition, but very much a physical one as well. People who are stressed often develop skin disorders, asthma, arthritis, niggling joint pains, hair loss, sleep disorders, poor appetite, weight loss or gain, and general exhaustion and irritability. All of these have their emotional, mental, and physical aspects and it is impossible to treat any of them in isolation. If we take any one of these conditions, we can probably treat the symptoms with painkillers, anti-depressants, or other medication. But that actually solves nothing. If we do not identify the cause, isolate the stress factors, and learn to cope better and improve our mental attitude, we will achieve nothing. Suppressing symptoms merely drives the problem underground, where it can fester and resurface later with much more serious implications.

So how stressed are you? What stresses you most? What are you going to do about it? How long will you put up with it? What do you think the long-term health implications are if you do nothing?

Consider first whether you are stressed by your work, what sort of stress you are under, how it might be manifesting itself, and what you can do about it.

Take a moment to fill in the questionnaire at Table 7.1, which will go some way to pinpointing your stress areas.

Each of the questions in the table fits into one of six categories:

1 Home and work;
2 Job satisfaction;

Table 7.1 Identifying your stress levels.

Tick the boxes to the right and score from 0-3	Stress free 0	Low stress 1	Medium stress 2	High stress 3
1 Not enough work to do	☐	☐	☐	☐
2 Too much work to do	☐	☐	☐	☐
3 Responsible for others and the way they work	☐	☐	☐	☐
4 Workplace politics	☐	☐	☐	☐
5 Changes in work patterns	☐	☐	☐	☐
6 Too many different roles	☐	☐	☐	☐
7 Work colleagues	☐	☐	☐	☐
8 Close friends at work	☐	☐	☐	☐
9 Remuneration	☐	☐	☐	☐
10 Environment	☐	☐	☐	☐
11 Overtime	☐	☐	☐	☐
12 Taking work home	☐	☐	☐	☐
13 Working hours – too long or unsociable	☐	☐	☐	☐
14 Being uncertain as to what is required	☐	☐	☐	☐
15 Having to make decisions	☐	☐	☐	☐
16 Deadlines	☐	☐	☐	☐
17 Boredom	☐	☐	☐	☐
18 Fear of being dismissed	☐	☐	☐	☐
19 Training	☐	☐	☐	☐
20 Under-utilized	☐	☐	☐	☐
21 My relationship with my direct boss	☐	☐	☐	☐
22 Thinking about work while away from it	☐	☐	☐	☐
23 No clear goals to work towards	☐	☐	☐	☐
24 Conflict at work	☐	☐	☐	☐
25 Approval, praise, and thanks	☐	☐	☐	☐
26 Job satisfaction	☐	☐	☐	☐
27 Being promoted too fast/too high	☐	☐	☐	☐
28 Giving presentations and speaking at meetings	☐	☐	☐	☐

(continued)

Table 7.1 *(continued).*

Tick the boxes to the right and score from 0-3	Stress free 0	Low stress 1	Medium stress 2	High stress 3
29 Being closely supervised	☐	☐	☐	☐
30 Promotion prospects	☐	☐	☐	☐
31 Support from my partner	☐	☐	☐	☐
32 Conflict with home	☐	☐	☐	☐
33 Outside interests conflicting with work	☐	☐	☐	☐
34 No regular assessments	☐	☐	☐	☐
35 Outside factors affecting work such as illness or finances	☐	☐	☐	☐
36 Morale of work colleagues	☐	☐	☐	☐

3 Position;
4 Responsibility;
5 Working pressure;
6 Work relationships.

1. Home and work

This is for questions 12, 22, 31, 32, 33, and 35.

If you have a stress score of over 12 for these six questions you should be thinking more about separating out work from your home life. There should be firm boundaries between the two. A score of between 8 and 12 indicates that you are showing some stress signs and need to look a little more closely at this issue. A score of under 8 shows that you seem to be managing successfully to keep the two apart.

2. Job satisfaction

This is for questions 9, 10, 20, 26, 30, and 18.

A score higher than 12 indicates low job satisfaction. You need to consider how highly praised and valued you are, and if you decide it is not highly enough, you need to question whether you are in the right job or working to the right levels of satisfaction. A score between 8 and 12 shows that you could do with being more satisfied and need to look at this area. If you scored under 8, you seem to be enjoying work.

3. Position

This is for questions 6, 5, 14, 17, 23, and 34.

A score higher than 12 reveals that you need to clear up any misunderstandings about your role. What does your job description say? Reaffirm your position with your immediate boss and keep it clearly defined. If you achieved a score between 8 and 12 you still need to be clearer about your position. A score below 8 shows that you have obviously well defined your position and are happy with it.

4. Responsibility

This is for questions 3, 4, 15, 24, 28, and 29.

A score higher than 12 shows that you seem to be stressed by the level of responsibilities you have. Perhaps too much is expected of you or you have been promoted to a post that you are not ready for yet – perhaps you are unqualified for it. You should seek retraining or support from colleagues. If you scored between 8 and 12, there are problems and you need to look closely at this area. A score below 8 indicates that you appear to be happy with the level of responsibility you hold.

5. Working pressure

This is for questions 1, 2, 11, 13, 16, and 27.

A score higher than 12 would indicate you simply have too much work to do. You need to look at delegating or shedding some of your work load. A score between 8 and 12 shows that you are still under too much strain and need to look at this area closely. If you scored under 8 you obviously have enough to do, unless you find question 1 a problem, in which case you have too little to do and should seek an increase in your work load or another form of employment.

6. Work relationships

This is for questions 7, 8, 19, 21, 25, and 36.

A score higher than 12 shows that there is obviously severe conflict at work and you need to get immediate support from senior staff to deal with this. If you scored between 8 and 12 there is obvious tension and you need to look at this area closely. If your score was below 8 you appear to get on well with your work colleagues and find your working environment happy and relatively stress free.

ELIMINATING STRESS FROM WORK

Once we have isolated our problem areas at work, we can do something about them. Here are some tips to help you eliminate stress from your work and be more relaxed about it.

» Be assertive. If you feel under stress, then say so. Express your feelings at work. Be honest with people and do not bottle things up.
» Be clear about what is work and what is not. Separate your work from your home life. Do not take work home with you – and do not take your home problems to work.
» Be comfortable. Make sure your office chair is right for you. Make sure your working environment is warm enough or cool enough. Have whatever you need to be comfortable enough to get the job done properly, but not so comfortable that you fall asleep.
» Be committed. If you have chosen to do the job then get on with it. If you find you cannot do it, then change jobs.
» Be focused at work. You are there to do a task, so do it. You are not there for the social life, the free pens, the company car, or the fine view from the office window.
» Be healthy. Make sure the job is adding to your health and not detracting from it. This applies to your moral and emotional health just as much as your physical health. If the job you are doing goes against the grain of your personal views and beliefs you will suffer stress.
» Be organized. Plan your work load, your desk, your diary, your day. Do not put things off, do things when you are supposed to do them.
» Be safe. Make sure you are working in an environment that is suitable. Check your Health and Safety regulations.
» Do not take on too much. You are not superhuman. If you have junior staff, use them. Delegate. Learn to say no to too much work.
» Eat sensibly. You should gear your food intake to the type of work you have to do. If you are a manual worker you need more calories. If your important meetings are in the afternoon do not have a heavy or alcoholic lunch. Do not binge on high calorie snacks and watch

your intake of coffee and other caffeine drinks. Watch how much you smoke. Be aware of your drinking habits and patterns.

» Have a fixed working day – and stick to it. Go home when you are supposed to. If you say you are going to stop at a certain time, make sure you do.

» Have a life. Make sure you do not spend all your time working, thinking about work, talking about work. Have some friends who do not work in the same business. Have hobbies and social activities that take you away from your work areas.

» Have goals. Make sure the job you are doing furthers your personal life goals and that you are not just filling in time waiting for something better to turn up. Make plans to make sure it does if that is the case.

» Take breaks. You need to get away from work every now and again. This might be every few hours, days, weeks, or months but no one should expect you to work without suitable and beneficial breaks.

» Work to live, not the other way round. When all is said and done, it is only a job. It might be very important to you – but your health, happiness, and welfare come first.

» You are entitled to support. If you need to retrain, develop new skills, improve, get help, or even just talk about work problems, then you should be able to enlist support from the senior staff above you.

Stress is an attitude problem. Two people faced with the same stressful situation will approach it and experience it completely differently. One might be fired up by it and see it as a learning challenge and exciting, while the other would be daunted, frightened, and will see it as something to be avoided at all costs. The difference – attitude. And we can change our attitude. We can change the way we view the world and its challenges. We can change our perception of what is stressful and what is exhilarating. For someone like me, climbing a mountain would be extremely stressful – I get the shakes just thinking about being up high, but public speaking holds absolutely no terror whatsoever. Now mountaineers like heights, but might well find that giving the lecture tour afterwards about how they climbed K2 would be completely daunting. Different strokes for different folks. Of course, we cannot all become mountaineers or public speakers overnight. There is no magic switch. But there are ways of changing our attitude even if that merely means being assertive enough to say "No, thank you but I won't join you on your trip to Everest."

Stressed people often suffer from what is known as "rigid thinking." This occurs in people who have definite fixed ideas about what life should be, what their role in it is, how others should be, what others should do. It is easy to identify rigid thinkers by their overuse of certain words – should, must, have to, got to. They will accost you in the office and declare, "You must do this because . . . " Rather than "It might be best if you did this because . . . ". We all suffer from it to some extent, but if we want to cut down on the stress and the way it affects us, we have to learn to be more flexible in our thinking – flexible thinking leads to flexible bodies. (Notice I said "have to learn" there, wrong. I should have said "might be best" instead. Notice I said "I should have said". . . Once you are aware of the danger signs you will realize how easy it is to think rigidly.)

Here are the top twenty tips for freeing up your mental approach to life, work and everything.

1 **Be aware of what you are**. You are a complex being made up of emotions, physical parts, mental processes, and a spiritual quality. We all need to devote some time to all the four aspects of ourselves. We need to express our emotions and have lots of them; take care of our bodies and maintain them well; develop, expand, and utilize our mental processes and constantly stretch them; and we need to have a spiritual dimension to our lives. This does not mean belonging to an organized religion, it might be as simple as taking a delight and wonder in nature, or as complicated as taking on an entire belief system such as Catholicism or Hinduism.

2 **Be aware of who you are**. Know your limitations. Do not take on too much. Be prepared to fail occasionally. Forgive yourself when you foul up. Laugh at yourself (a lot) when you take yourself seriously. Stop making excuses.

3 **Be nice to yourself**. Take some time for yourself occasionally. Reward yourself, you deserve it. Treat yourself, you have earned it. Pamper yourself, you need it. Do not wait for others to approve of you, approve of yourself. Do not wait for others to love you, love yourself. Do not wait for others to take you out, take yourself out. Enjoy all you can. Have fun. Have more fun. The more relaxed we

are, both mentally and physically, the better companions we are, the better we can cope with life and the better able we are to help others. The nicer we are to ourselves the more likely we are to want to be nice to others. When we are relaxed and happy, others will want to be around us more.

4 **Check the mechanics**. We are complex, fragile organisms that needs a lot of care and maintenance. Look after the mechanics of your body. Without proper sleep, food, and exercise it will deteriorate more quickly than it should. The human body does not come with a maintenance manual, so you have to do a little research of your own. Be prepared for changes within the body and put right anything as soon as it goes wrong, rather than wait until the entire system collapses. Looking after your body well is not selfish or vain - it is sound practical common sense.

5 **Develop yourself**. You are not a static being. You are growing and changing all the time. Develop new interests and new friends constantly. Purge old interests and old situations if they no longer suit you or fulfil you. Learn to move on. When something has been done to death you can drop it. Always be ready to explore, to try new experiences, new situations. Study new things. Improve your education. Read lots. Be adaptable and eager to try anything (except incest and morris dancing, as Sir Thomas Beecham wisely said!). If you do not try new things you simply will have no idea whether you like them or not - and do not try saying that you are not the sort of person who would not like this or that - you will never know until you try. Be flexible in your thinking. Do not get stuck in routines or habits. The more unconventional, unpredictable, and unstuck we are, the more we develop and grow mentally.

6 **Don't take life personally**. All life is a mixture of good and bad. When bad things happen to you - as they have done, do, and will continue to do - accept them as part of life. They have not been inflicted on you deliberately, or as some form of divine punishment. It is just life being colourful and varied. If only good things happened, we would never learn anything and life would be very dull. We all have a little misfortune from time to time. And we all need to work through it and learn from it.

7 **Everything changes**. Whatever your situation is now, it will change. There is nothing that you can do about that, so just accept that change is inescapable. When we fear change, or try to avoid it or resist it, our mental processes become clogged. When we accept change as inevitable, then we can react to it as exciting and our mental processes remain clear and relaxed.

8 **Express your feelings**. You have them and you are allowed to express them. Learn to talk more about how you feel. Be honest with others about your feelings. Do not go along with others just because it makes things easier – the repercussions will be worse for you and for them in the long run. Express both the positive and the negative. If you feel irritated say so. If you feel happy say so. Learn to be assertive and say when you do not want to do something, or when you feel that a situation is wrong for you.

9 **Know what you want**. Look ahead and plan where you want to be and what you want to be doing. Give your life direction. Think about yourself and what is good for you and work towards it. Try not to set your sights too high, but be realistic and allow for a change in plans or fortunes. Make your goals flexible and have both long-term and short-term plans.

10 **Learn to laugh more**. Laughter, research has shown, can help us recover more quickly from illness, allow us to cope better with life's dramas, and generally improve our health. Check how often you laugh – not just a mere smile or a chuckle, but a good belly laugh, a guffawing raucous laughter that brings tears to your eyes and has you feeling helpless – literally rolling on the floor with laughter. Go out of your way to encounter situations that you know will make you laugh. It does not all have to be so serious.

11 **Look for choice**. There are always two ways (at least) to do anything or to approach any situation. When we have choice we feel free and in control. Accept nothing at face value. Always ask what the choices are, and look for the choices in any situation. Nothing in life is set in concrete – there is always an alternative. The alternative may not be pleasant or acceptable, and we may discard it, but at least we shall feel as if we had a choice, and thus feel freer and more in control.

12 **Manage your relationships**. Unless you put in some time and effort, relationships will decay and fall apart. You have to do some work. Think about your relationships – not just with your partner but also with your friends, work colleagues, acquaintances, close family, relatives, and neighbours. If you are unhappy with any of them, then work out what you can do to change them, or improve them. Be aware that all relationships are organic – they grow and they wither. All relationships can end, so be prepared: nothing is for ever. If a relationship is going nowhere, then it might be better to terminate it rather than let things drag on. All relationships are two-way things, you have to take the other people into consideration; they are not there just for you.

13 **Manage your time effectively**. Allow time for leisure interests, family, love, fun, work, travel, study, yourself, solitude, rest, and more fun. Allot time schedules for these areas and make sure you have a little of all of them. Allow some time for future planning and to check that you are managing your time effectively.

14 **Set yourself standards**. This does not go against the advice about not being rigid in your thinking. We need moral standards and intellectual standards. Strive always for quality and improvement in your intellectual standards so that you remain interesting and vibrant. Set your moral standards high so you value yourself as a human being and can take pride in your achievements and moral health. Set your life standards for simplicity and happiness, rather than for work and acquisitions. Accept only the best for yourself.

15 **Go round, not through**. If you habitually encounter situations where you feel intensely frustrated and unable to change anything, maybe it might be helpful to avoid them or change your response. Instead of seeing situations as frustrating, try to see them as challenging. You do not have problems, you have learning experiences. You do not have frustrations, you have unique opportunities to improve your skills and abilities. There are times when we are all frustrated – we cannot get what we want, or get people to do what we want, or get a situation to our liking – but good mental relaxation is all about how we approach that frustration and how we handle it. If our attitude is relaxed and we accept that frustration is inevitable, we can cope better.

16 **Do not demand**. Allow life to work around you rather than trying to bludgeon it into submission. Change what you can and let go of the rest. There are many things outside your control and they can be ignored. What is within your control can be dealt with.

17 **Stop trying to be perfect**. It is more relaxed and helpful to accept that we are human beings – full of faults and foibles. Stop thinking of yourself as a flawed being, and accept the "negative" bits as part of a well-rounded personality. Accept yourself as you are. If you took away all that you consider to be "bad," you would not be the wonderful human being you are. It is OK to improve; it is unhelpful to try to be perfect.

18 **Take responsibility**. It is no one's fault you are the way you are. If you could get together everyone you blame, and tell them off, or punish them, or rage at them, it would not change a thing about you. If you blame other people, or life, or events, you will not do anything about the way you are – you will remain a victim. If you take responsibility, you can take positive steps to change anything you consider needs changing, and then get on with your life. Do not dwell on the past – it cannot be changed. Dwell on the future – it *can* be changed.

19 **Take stock of yourself**. Look in a mirror and see where you are at in your life. What age are you? What does that mean? How do you feel? How healthy are you? How relaxed? How much fun are you having? Do you work too hard? How are your relationships? Are you getting enough or too much sex? What are you scared of? Do you like "you?"

20 **Where are you rushing to**? Life is not a destination, it is a journey. Take time out to enjoy the trip occasionally. Look around you. Count your blessings. Take some time to savor life, to enjoy the quieter bits. Put your feet up from time to time and allow yourself to do absolutely nothing except watch the scenery go by.

Work, work, work

We all need to work, to be useful and productive, creative and occupied, but why do we work? Do we work to live? Or live to work? Without leisure time for hobbies, outside interests, and enjoyment, we become very dull indeed. Recent research in America has shown that people recovering from heart attacks made better progress and had fewer subsequent attacks if they followed a three-pronged approach to life. They needed to learn a meditation/relaxation technique. They needed a belief system of some sort to support them. And thirdly they needed to belong to a social group of some sort – and it could be as simple as going to night classes or having a few friends drop in for tea on a regular basis. The evidence also suggested that if we practice these three things in advance, our likelihood of living to a ripe old age is greatly enhanced. What are you waiting for?

Hobbies

Terrible word, isn't it? Hobbies. Why not call them leisure activities. Your leisure activities could literally save your life. So what leisure activities do you have?

» Make a list of all the things that you would like to do but have never got round to – and then list why not.
» List all the things you have done over the last ten or twenty years that you really enjoyed, but maybe do not do quite so often now. And then write down the reasons why you do not do them now.
» Take one item from each list and do it now – and then work your way through each list over the next year, doing them all. Go for it!

Getting physical

We have looked at sorting out stress levels, we shall look at eating habits in the next section – what's next? Ah, physical activity I'm afraid. This is the one most people report a problem with. They *want* to do more physically, have all the right ideas about it, are initially motivated and encouraged – but it all tails off back into sedentary hell. So how can we keep it up? How can we find a long-term solution?

We often simply do not have time to exercise. There just is not the time to get to a gym. So we need to find ways of being more active without resorting to weight training, jogging, aerobics, or cycling machines. They all have their place and are an invaluable part of exercise – but not for people who simply cringe at the thought. Here are a few ideas that might inspire you and make you think about physical activities in a new light.

» **Gardening.** Get out there and weed, prune, cut, strim, hack, slash, weed again, and rake. You will be doing aerobics, weight lifting, stretching, and strengthening all the time. As a result you will be fitter, get fresh air, get rid of a lot of stress, have a fabulous garden, and please your partner. Try to do everything by hand as far as possible – sitting on a mower gives you no benefit you at all, but walking behind a push-along mower does.

» **Walking.** This is still the best form of exercise there is. It is inexpensive – OK, so you have to have shoes – it increases your heart and lung rate, it is easy on the joints but exercises them, it lifts your mood, it gets you lots of fresh air, and it is extremely pleasurable. You can walk to work if possible, or if you go by car you could at least park a little way away and walk the rest. If you go by subway, try getting off a stop or two before you need to and walking in. Half an hour of brisk walking burns around 200–300 calories, and you get to enjoy the scenery.

» **Bicycling.** When we were kids we rode bikes all the time and we were fit and active. Somewhere along the way we lost the bike, and gained the paunch or the spare tire. Get a bike again and get out there and conquer a few hills. Bike technology has made some terrific leaps in the past decade and modern technology means that it is all fun now – mountain bikes are easy to ride, and pretty cool, image-wise.

» **Housework and decorating.** Just being busy around the home can work off quite a few calories as well as stretching us considerably. Try running up the stairs instead of walking up them. Dusting and vacuuming can all keep us fit and active – just so long as we put some effort into it. And when that painting needs doing, do not get someone in – do it yourself. Being active is a major key to good health and body care.

CASE STUDY - ROBERT PATERSON'S STORY

I was coming back from Havana, an international investment banker, looking for another job in the City. I was weighing in at over 22 stone. My chances of getting another job, the way I looked, were slender. Worse, even if I got another job, the doctors had been telling me, for years, that unless I lost some weight I would not see out a normal career, let alone old age.

I had, over the years, tried many different diets. They all worked. They all succeeded in getting weight off, but none of them succeeded in enabling me to *keep* it off. So, rather than go for another crash diet, I decided to analyse why anyone, including myself, becomes overweight. I came up with only four reasons:

1 **Genetics** - nothing anyone can do about that, at present. It is like getting a bad hand at cards, but you still have to play the hand. Being genetically pre-disposed to obesity does not mean that you are incapable of having a healthy life. There are excellent scientific studies on this!
2 **Nutrition** - too much nutrition, not enough exercise.
3 **Exercise** - too much exercise, not enough nutrition!
4 **Mindset** - the key factor that is so readily overlooked. Many will say if you want to lose weight and get fitter, it is just a question of will power. I can assure you that most overweight, unfit individuals have buckets of will power. That is not what enables you to succeed, long-term.

Armed with this information I decided to develop my understanding of the three areas which I could manage - nutrition, exercise, and mindset.

Where was I to go for help?

The first thing I tried was some friendly and well known "slimmers' clubs." All of them were most welcoming - especially as I was the token male. And that is just the point. I wanted to belong to a group. As a man, I felt I did not belong there. Besides, most of the people I met, at these meetings, had a totally different lifestyle to my own. They could get down to the church hall every Wednesday night. They had a set pattern to the day. They had time often to shop and cook. My life revolved around my work. Tight schedules, business travel and entertaining - how could I cope with this sort of programme?

I joined a gym. Fine, while I was around the area. But for an executive how often is one around and how much time is available for exercise in an average business day? Not much, I concluded.

Then I discovered, partly from looking back at what had and what had not worked for me, that all the diet programmes I could find really concentrated on one, or at the most two, key areas of weight management. They either focused on nutrition (slimmers' clubs), or exercise (gyms and health clubs). Hardly anyone touched on mindset.

What was worse is that each area could give you *their* formula for how to manage *your* weight. Frankly, you can follow someone else's program for just so long - being human we tend to go back to our old tried and tested methods - and that is where most diets fail. You just cannot stick to them. Why? Because they do not address all the issues that need to be tackled and they do not make the whole package a personal one, modeled around your own lifestyle. You see, someone may want to run a marathon, and the next guy wants to walk the dog three times a week. They may both want to get healthier and fitter, but their ultimate goals are totally different. It is self-evident that their nutrition and exercise need to be different too!

In some desperation, I decided that the only way forward was to "invent" my own diet. And that is when I started to look at what skills I had for doing this. I knew how to run a company - but could my body be managed along similar lines? I started putting this to the test.

First, I took on a group of consultants to help me run the business. They included a nutritionist (State Registered Dietician), a personal trainer, and a life coach (for the mindset). I told them what my goals and objectives were and I wrote my own "business plan" around my body. This included a "history of the company." What had I done in managing this business before, and what could I learn from those experiences? I did a SWOT analysis - was I a fair weather sportsman? Was that one of my weaknesses? And could I manage time well? Yes! That was one of the strengths. I had been a time manager, in my business life, for years.

Now I could see how my business skills could be used in the management of my body. I went further - I realized that a culture change would be necessary, painful as it may be. But I had managed culture change before. I knew that just like a business, my actions in managing my body would affect others. I needed to manage those people's expectations. How was I going to persuade my old drinking buddies that I was about to change? What benefits would my partner get out of the process? Other than being forced to give up good restaurant eating - hardly a benefit!

And then there was the management of the business. What did I really want to produce? Driving down my stock levels (reducing weight) would turn me into a more efficient company with a healthier bank balance - but what was I going to produce? I decided I would be an athlete, albeit an amateur one! I set my mind to running my first marathon, then my second, then triathletics and now bikehiking, a charitable event I set up with the Family Heart Association, as a way of giving something back, and literally ''walking the talk,'' at the same time - www.greatbikehike.co.uk

Time management was foremost in the skills that I brought to bear in running my body business. I knew there were certain vital areas that I had to cover in managing my body, all of which would be time related.

1 **Planning and doing exercise – regularly.** This was achieved by looking at that part of my day like a business meeting. I made it sacrosanct. I would get up 45 minutes earlier each day, much easier when I cut down on alcohol and went to bed just a little earlier! This also meant that I did not have to shower twice a day, as I would get straight out of bed, into my kit and my exercise routine and then under the shower. A huge time saving all round - and it ensured that I got most of my regular training done every day. Most people tend to train after work - this has the benefit of being a great stress reliever, but is more time-consuming than the morning routine and does not always guarantee success when a busy schedule gets in the way.

2 **Planning and cooking my meals.** I decided that I would plan my meals one week ahead then "batch cook," making double the quantity of any given recipe and freezing the result in meal-sized portions. It meant I only needed to cook once, or at most twice, per week. I also "invented" some really quick but healthy meals. These had some rules. They must never take more than 30 minutes to prepare and cook, because that was how long the alternative (a take-away pizza or an Indian meal) would take to deliver. They also had to be well-balanced and healthy, and all the ingredients had to be available at any late-night supermarket, because I needed to pick them up on the way home from work.

3 **Monitoring and measuring results.** You would not expect to change a corner-shop to a multinational enterprise overnight. Nor would you expect your body to perform like an Olympian in just a few weeks. Time management enabled me to take things at a gradual and steady pace. It took me six months training to run my first 10K race and a further 12 months after that before I ran my first marathon. I knew that my weight loss would be a similar exercise. Companies do not review their health and profitability on a daily basis – yet most weight managers jump on the bathroom scales and expect to get an instant result. When, in spite of doing everything right, the scales show a slight increase many give up and go back to their old habits. Would you do that in your business?

What were some of the other management skills I brought to my weight management business?

1 **The management of change.** Change is a four-step process – miss one of the steps and the result will be ultimate failure. These steps are:
   » dissatisfaction with the present position;
   » a clear and attractive vision of the future;
   » stepping stones between where you are today and the vision of where you want to be in the future; and

» an unshakeable belief that the process is possible and that crossing the stepping stones will get you there.

2 **Management of the "internal" self.** How good is your internal dialogue? Mine was worse than judge and jury put together. We all have rules for how we handle situations and I started to look at what sort of "culture" my body business had. If I had a young manager who was still learning the skills in running the business, would I pounce on him every time he made a mistake? What would that do to my business if I did? In the case of my body I would find myself being that "bullying manager" every time I "slipped" up. By taking the approach of the caring and educating line manager, I suddenly discovered that when I came off-track with my programme, I learnt from the process rather than beat myself up for getting it wrong.

Realizing the isolation that men experience when confronting weight management issues, and understanding how similar the process can be to running a company, I decided, based on my own success, to found *Warriors* – the only weight management programme in Britain for men.

Warriors

Warriors has been running for almost two years with excellent results. To begin with it has been London based, but on its second anniversary it is poised to expand into Manchester and Glasgow.

We run 10-week programmes that start with a one-day workshop, followed by a ten-day period spent developing the body "business plan," and after that we provide on-going support by e-mail on a weekly basis. Further assistance is also provided through personal trainers, life coaches, and nutritionists. Full details of the programme and how to book a course are available through the web site – www.warriors.org.uk

My book *Warriors*, published by Piatkus Books, is available from all major UK bookshops.

Key Concepts in Body Care

Medical language is complex, but the basic concepts, techniques and elements of body care, together with the principal treatments and philosophies which those who care about their bodies will encounter, are explained simply and directly in the ExpressExec glossary in this chapter.

The *Healthy People 2010: National Health Promotion and Disease Prevention Objectives* (see Chapter 9) document notes that up to 50% of chronic disease mortality is attributable to lifestyle factors that can be changed. For example, the Surgeon General's report states, "For two out of three adult Americans who do not smoke and do not drink excessively, one personal choice seems to influence long-term health prospects more than any other: what we eat."

GLOSSARY

Acupressure – Acupressure is based on the same ancient Chinese principles as acupuncture, but instead of using needles, finger pressure is used on specific body points. As with acupuncture, it is used to treat a variety of ailments, including relief from the pain of arthritis, menstrual cramps, muscle tension, and various other aches and pains. Acupressure is also used to improve overall health and well-being.

Acupuncture – Acupuncture originated in China over five thousand years ago. It is based on the belief that good health is determined by a balanced flow of *ch'i* (also referred to as *qi*), the life energy present in all living beings. According to acupuncture theory, ch'i circulates in the body along twelve major energy pathways, called *meridians*, each linked to specific internal organs and organ structures. There are over one thousand *acupoints* within the meridian system that can be stimulated to enhance the flow of ch'i. When special needles are inserted into these acupoints (just under the skin), they help to correct and rebalance the flow of energy, and consequently relieve pain and restore health.

Alexander Technique – The Alexander Technique stresses the importance of re-educating the muscular system as a means of achieving physical and mental well-being. Suffering from chronic voice loss, the actor F. Matthias Alexander developed this technique. Alexander teachers use hands-on guidance and verbal instruction to teach simple and efficient ways of relieving tension and stress by improving balance, posture, and co-ordination.

Applied kinesiology (touch for health) – Applied kinesiology can determine health imbalances in the body's organs and glands by identifying weaknesses in specific muscles. By stimulating or relaxing these key muscles, an applied kinesiologist can diagnose and resolve a variety of health problems.

Aromatherapy – Aromatherapy is a unique branch of herbal medicine that uses the medicinal properties found in the essential oils of various plants. Through a process of steam distillation or cold-pressing, the volatile constituents of the plant's oil (its essence) are extracted from its flowers, leaves, branches, or roots. The oils exert much of their therapeutic effect through their pharmacological properties and their small molecular size, making them one of the few therapeutic agents to penetrate the body tissues easily.

Ayurvedic medicine – Practiced in India for the past five thousand years, Ayurvedic medicine (meaning "science of life") is a comprehensive system of medicine that combines natural therapies with a highly personalized approach to the treatment of disease. Ayurvedic medicine places equal emphasis on body, mind, and spirit, and strives to restore the harmony of the individual.

"Disposition" is the keystone of Ayurvedic medicine, and refers to the overall health profile of the individual, including strengths and susceptibilities. Once established, it becomes the foundation for all clinical decisions. According to a person's metabolic body type (constitution), a specific treatment plan is designed to guide the individual back into harmony with his or her environment. This may include dietary changes, exercise, yoga, meditation, massage, herbal tonics, herbal sweat baths, medicated enemas, and medicated inhalations.

Bach flower remedies – The emotions play a crucial role in the health of the physical body. Flower remedies directly address a person's emotional state in order to help facilitate both psychological and physiological well-being. By balancing negative feelings and stress, flower remedies can effectively remove the emotional barriers to health and recovery.

Biofeedback training – Biofeedback training is a method of learning how to regulate consciously the normally unconscious bodily functions (such as breathing, heart rate, and blood pressure) in order to improve overall health. It refers to any process that measures and reports back immediate information about the biological system of the person being monitored so that he or she can learn to influence that system consciously. Biofeedback is particularly useful for learning to reduce stress, eliminating headaches, controlling asthmatic attacks, reconditioning injured muscles, and relieving pain.

Biological dentistry – Biological dentistry treats the teeth, jaw, and related structures with specific regard to how treatment will affect the entire body. Biological dentistry stresses the use of non-toxic restoration materials for dental work, and focuses on the unrecognized impact that dental toxins and hidden dental infections have on overall health.

Bodywork – The term bodywork refers to therapies such as massage, deep tissue manipulation, movement awareness, and energy balancing, which are employed to improve the structure and functions of the human body. Bodywork in all its forms helps to reduce pain, soothe injured muscles, stimulate blood and lymphatic circulation, and promote deep relaxation.

Chi Kung – Chi Kung (also known as *qigong*) is an ancient Chinese exercise that stimulates and balances the flow of ch'i, or vital life energy, along the acupuncture meridians (energy pathways). Like acupuncture and traditional Chinese medicine, the Chi Kung tradition emphasizes the importance of teaching the patient how to remain well. In China, the various methods of Chi Kung form the nucleus of a national self-care system of health maintenance and personal development. Chi Kung cultivates inner strength, calms the mind, and restores the body to its natural state of health by maintaining the optimum functioning of the body's self-regulating systems.

Chelation therapy – Chelation (key-LAY-shun) comes from the Greek word *chelein* meaning "to claw". Chelation therapy is a safe and effective method for drawing toxins and metabolic wastes from the bloodstream. Chelating agents administered intravenously have been proven to increase blood flow and remove arterial plaque. Chelation therapy can help reverse atherosclerosis, can prevent heart attacks and strokes, and is used as an alternative to bypass surgery and angioplasty.

Chiropractic – Chiropractic is concerned with the relationship of the spinal column and the musculoskeletal structures of the body to the nervous system. Proper alignment of the spinal column is essential for optimum health because the spinal column acts as the central switching organization for the nervous system. When there is nerve interference caused by misalignments in the spine, known as *subluxations*, pain can occur and the body's defences can be diminished. By adjusting the spinal joints to remove subluxations, normal nerve function can be restored.

Colon therapy – The colon, along with the skin, kidneys, and lungs, is a major organ for eliminating bodily waste. The healthy function of the colon is essential for good digestion and the proper absorption of nutrients. If bowel movements are not consistent, waste products and toxins are not eliminated in a proper manner, and ill health can result. Colon therapy uses a series of colonic water flushes to clean and detoxify the lower intestine and aid in the reconstitution of beneficial intestinal flora.

Craniosacral therapy – Craniosacral therapy manipulates the bones of the skull to treat a range of conditions, from headache and ear infections to stroke, spinal cord injury, and cerebral palsy. For decades various forms of cranial manipulation have been used to improve overall body functioning, and today craniosacral therapy is gaining acceptance by health professionals world-wide as a successful treatment.

Detoxification therapy – Each year people are exposed to thousands of toxic chemicals and pollutants in the earth's atmosphere, water, food, and soil. These pollutants manifest themselves in a variety of symptoms, including decreased immune function, neurotoxicity, hormonal dysfunction, psychological disturbances, and even cancer. Detoxification therapy, combined with special cleansing diets or juice and water fasts, helps to rid the body of chemicals and pollutants and can facilitate a return to health.

Diet – A dietician will pay attention not only to what we eat but also to how it is grown or reared; what chemicals were used in its production; how it is stored and processed; how it is cooked and prepared; and even how it is served.

Environmental medicine – Environmental medicine explores the role of dietary and environmental allergens in health and illness. Factors such as dust, moulds, chemicals, and certain foods may cause allergic reactions that can dramatically influence diseases ranging from asthma and hay fever to headaches and depression. Virtually any chronic physical or mental illness may be improved by the care of a physician competent in this field.

Enzyme therapy – For every chemical reaction that occurs in the body, enzymes provide the stimulus. Enzymes are substances that make life possible, they help build the body from proteins, carbohydrates, and fats. The body may have the raw building materials, but without the enzymes, it cannot begin. Enzyme therapy can be an important first step in restoring health and well-being by helping to remedy digestive problems. Plant enzymes and pancreatic enzymes are used in complementary ways to improve digestion and absorption of essential nutrients. Treatment includes enzyme supplements, coupled with a healthy diet that features whole foods.

Fasting – Fasting is a low-cost, effective therapy for a wide range of conditions, including hypertension, headaches, allergies, and arthritis. By relieving the body of the task of digesting foods, fasting allows the system to rid itself of toxins while facilitating healing. Fasting should only be done over very short periods – never more than two days without medical supervision.

Homeopathy – The word homeopathy derives from the Greek words *homoios*, meaning "similar", and *pathos*, meaning "suffering". Homeopathic remedies are generally dilutions of natural substances from plants, minerals, and animals. Based on the principle of "like cures like", these remedies specifically match different symptom patterns or "profiles" of illness, and act to stimulate the body's natural healing response.

Hydrotherapy – Hydrotherapy is the use of water, ice, steam, and hot and cold temperatures to maintain and restore health. Treatments include full-body immersion, steam baths, saunas, hip baths, colonic irrigation, and the application of hot and/or cold compresses. Hydrotherapy is effective for treating a wide range of conditions and can easily be used in the home as part of a self-care program.

Hypnotherapy – For thousands of years the power of suggestion has played a major role in healing in cultures as varied as ancient Greece, Persia, and India. Hypnotherapy uses both the power of suggestion and trance-like states to access the deepest levels of the mind to effect positive changes in a person's behavior, and to treat a range of health conditions, including migraines, ulcers, respiratory conditions, tension headaches, and even warts.

Massage – There are many different types of massage, from very passive and gentle to extremely deep and active. Massage can be used to help patients recovering from operations, to help sports people improve their efficiency, soothing pain, aiding relaxation, helping people back to general fitness, reducing strain in soft tissues, cleansing bodily tissues, improving circulation, easing muscular aches and strains. Some forms, such as Swedish massage, are intended as an alternative to exercise while others, such as *shiatsu*, are healing in their approach.

Meditation – Meditation can be broadly defined as any activity that keeps the attention pleasantly anchored in the present moment. When the mind is calm and focused in the present, it is neither reacting to memories of the past nor being preoccupied with plans for the future, two major sources of chronic stress known to affect health.

Meditation is a safe and simple way to balance the physical, emotional, and mental states. It is easily learned and has been used as an aid in treating stress and pain management. It has also been employed as part of an overall treatment for other conditions, including hypertension and heart disease.

Neuro-linguistic programming (NLP) – Neuro-linguistic programming focuses on how people learn, communicate, change, grow, and heal. 'Neuro' refers to the way the brain works and how human thinking demonstrates consistent and detectable patterns. 'Linguistic' refers to the verbal and non-verbal expressions of the brain's thinking patterns. 'Programming' refers to how these patterns are recognized and understood by the mind and how they can be altered, allowing a person to make better choices in behavior and health.

NLP has provided positive results for people suffering from various conditions, including allergies, arthritis, Parkinson's disease, and migraine headaches.

Osteopathy – Osteopathy considers and treats the patient as a whole rather than narrowly focusing on a specific ailment. It is a form of physical medicine that helps restore the structural balance of the musculoskeletal system. Combining joint manipulation, physical therapy, and postural re-education, osteopathy is effective in treating spinal and joint difficulties, arthritis, digestive disorders, menstrual problems, and chronic pain.

T'ai chi – T'ai chi is a Chinese system of very gentle movements to encourage complete and overall exercise. It has two forms long and short which can take between five minutes and half an hour to complete. All the movements are gentle and are designed to be carried out in a small space, so you can do this at home or in the office. In China it is a national activity and often incorporated quite naturally into the working day t'ai breaks.

Traditional Chinese medicine (TCM) – Traditional Chinese medicine is an ancient method of health care that combines the use of medicinal herbs, acupuncture, food therapy, massage, and therapeutic exercise. The philosophy of TCM is preventative and makes a point of educating the patient with regard to lifestyle so that the patient can assist in his or her own healing process. The TCM practitioner educates the patient about diet, exercise, stress management, rest, and relaxation.

Yoga – Yoga means "union": the integration of physical, mental, and spiritual energies that enhance health and well-being. It was first written about by Patanjali in the second century BC in the Yoga Sutras. Yoga teaches a basic principle of mind/body unity: if the mind is chronically restless and agitated, the health of the body will be compromised, and if the body is in poor health, mental strength and clarity will be adversely affected. The practices of yoga can counter these ill effects, restoring mental and physical health. The most basic yoga is Hatha yoga, which is a series of movements known as *asanas* (postures) designed to keep the body supple and fit. They can be learnt by anyone quite simply.

TECHNIQUES

Exercise Lite

Being inactive is a major contributory factor in coronary heart disease, osteoporosis, hypertension, colon cancer, anxiety, depression, non-insulin dependent diabetes, and some cancers. Who says so? The Office for Disease Prevention and Health Promotion (ODPHP) which is located within the Office of Public Health and Science, Office of the Secretary, US Department of Health and Human Services (HHS) – see Chapter 9 for web addresses.

The American College of Sports Medicine suggests that few people in the US are physically active because previous health efforts to promote physical activity have over-emphasized the importance of high intensity exercise. There is a perception that only vigorous continuous physical activity has any benefit, but the scientific evidence seems to point to regular, moderate-intensity physical activity actually providing greater and more substantial health benefits. So tear up the gym membership and do some heavy gardening instead.

There is a campaign in the US to get people up off the sofa and back to doing something active. It is called Exercise Lite and its aim is not to get the entire population racing around the track or jogging fifty miles a day, but instead to do something fairly active a few times a week.

Exercise Lite is a baseline program. The most dramatic health benefits come when you go from doing nothing to this kind of moderate exercise and enhanced general activity level. Note that although you may feel tired at the end of a day of shopping, cooking, and chasing after your kids, this does not constitute an adequate "workout". More is better, and you may decide to do even more exercise when you see how much better you feel after a few weeks of "exercise lite."

But what is "lite" and what is heavy? Doing the ironing might seem exhausting but it is really quite lite whereas scaling Mount Everest is very heavy indeed.

Judge your activity by the following scale. If you

» sit, stand, drive, sew, iron or cook; your activity level is very light and you burn few calories;
» clean the house, take care of children, play golf and walk for less than two miles; your activity is light;

» work hard in the garden, cycle, play tennis, walk for more than two miles or dance; your activity level is moderate;
» indulge in manual labour, play basketball or soccer, or climb; your activity level is heavy.

The higher the activity level the more calories you burn and the better your physical fitness.

How much exercise is enough?

But how much exercise do we need to take in order to stay healthy? It would seem that to gain moderate benefits we need to engage in at least 30 minutes of moderate to vigorous physical activity most days. That does not mean once a week but *most* days. This could be as simple as three brisk ten-minute walks during the day, or half an hour of jogging. Even moderate exercise increases fitness, keeps blood pressure down, and helps to build muscle and lose body fat.

Motivation

I know; most of us would rather do something else, but if we do not take exercise our health will suffer. Try keeping an activity diary for one week only. Note down everything you do - and for how long. You may well be so surprised and shocked at just how much time you spend sitting down that you may not need any further motivation to get up and take some exercise.

Most people report that doing exercise on their own is de-motivating - so get a friend or partner to help. Doing anything in company is more pleasurable than going it alone. Even a gentle stroll - or should that be a brisk walk? - will be more enjoyable with a friend or partner than just walking on your own. You could even hold mini-business meetings with colleagues while walking - try it and you might like the idea.

Get five friends to agree to walk together once or twice a week. You all pay a nominal sum into a kitty and whoever has missed the fewest sessions gets the money at the end of the month - or whatever. You can work out your own financial motivator.

> **Caution**
>
> If you are under- or over-weight, suffer from high blood pressure or any form of heart disorder, are aged 40 or over, or if you have any health concerns, then consult a qualified medical practitioner before embarking on any regime of physical fitness.

Good food guide

Are we taking on board the right sort of fuel to keep us healthy and fit and active and strong? Without a healthy balanced diet no-one will ever achieve the right levels of body care. A balanced diet can:

- » improve your general fitness;
- » restore your energy levels;
- » nourish your skin and hair;
- » uplift your mood;
- » help your circulation;
- » reinforce your immune system;
- » tone muscle and internal organs; and
- » generally make you feel better able to cope with whatever life can throw at you.

Good healthy eating at regular, sensible times is probably one of the greatest relaxations we can enjoy – and one that we simply do not indulge ourselves in often enough. We only have to look to Europe and the Mediterranean countries to see what a pleasure meals with the family can be. There are a few guidelines to healthy eating:

- » buy organic if you can (ideally, grow your own);
- » cut down on processed food – pies, sausages, processed meats;
- » do not eat alone if you can avoid it – good conversation is a marvellous appetite stimulator;
- » eat fresh food rather than packaged, tinned, frozen, or dried;
- » eat less fat – especially butter, cheese, full-fat milk, cream, red meats, and fried foods; eat low-fat foods instead – low-fat yoghurts, margarine, semi-skimmed milk; eat more non-oily fish, and steam and bake meals rather than frying them;

» eat lots of roughage – cereals, peas, beans, fruit, vegetables, pasta;
» eat regularly – three main meals a day at set times and only very light snacks in between;
» switch snacks from chocolate and crisps to fruit and raw vegetables, such as carrot sticks;
» eat smaller quantities at each meal;
» make food preparation and cooking part of your lifestyle so you can enjoy the process; for instance bake your own bread: enjoy your food;
» be sure to eat some fresh green salad or vegetables at least once a day;
» reduce your consumption of mood-altering foods and drinks – sugar, salt, caffeine, alcohol; and
» take your time over your food, and always aim to eat sitting down at a table.

Being overweight

Simply being overweight puts you at risk. It is a proven factor in:

» heart disease;
» diabetes;
» narrowing and hardening of the arteries;
» high blood pressure;

Table 8.1   Ideal weights according to height.

Men	
5ft–5ft 4in	120–130lbs
5ft 5in–5ft 7in	130–140lbs
5ft 8in–5ft 10in	140–155lbs
5ft 11in–6ft 1in	155–165lbs
Women	
5ft–5ft 2in	105–115 lbs
5ft 3in–5ft 5in	115–125 lbs
5ft 6in–5ft 8in	125–135 lbs
5ft 9in–6ft	135–150 lbs

» strokes;
» kidney disease;
» poor blood supply to internal organs; and
» arthritis.

Being 10% or more over your ideal weight counts as being overweight, and more than 20% as obese. Table 8.1 shows the ideal weights for men and women, according to their heights.

Resources for Body Care

There are many excellent reference works which describe body care techniques. This chapter identifies the most relevant resources in books and Websites on health issues and on body care matters.

Body fat has been given a bad press. No one wants it, and countless millions are spent on diets and exercise programs designed to get rid of it. But fat - or white adipose tissue - is actually a vital organ that boosts the immune system, produces hormones and governs our energy metabolism.

> "Fat is definitely good for us. The old view that fat does nothing is wrong. It does much more than we think. It protects muscles, produces a whole lot of hormones and changes the metabolism of the female sex hormone oestrogen. It is just an excess of fat that isn't good and is a health risk."
>
> *Professor Andrew Prentice, Medical Research Council*

BOOKS

Whether you believe that body fat is good or bad, you will be able to find a book or a website that supports your belief. More has probably been written about medicine and health than about any other subject. Most book stores, including on-line stores, offer very many titles on aspects of health. The following books and websites all offer some specific information on aspects of body care which have been covered in this book, or which anyone who is aware of the importance of body care may be interested in. Read and learn, but remember that reading was not on the list of healthy exercises!

Maslach C. with Leiter M.P. (1997) *The Truth About Burnout: How Organizations Cause Personal Stress and What to Do About It*, Jossey-Bass Inc., USA.

Burnout has reached epidemic proportions in the US. Based on an extensive study of burnout victims, this book exposes the current crisis and offers methods of prevention. After identifying the source of the problem, the authors offer specific prescriptive measures - for assessment, goal-setting, crisis intervention, and prevention of future burnout.

O'Neil J.R. (1994) *The Paradox of Success: When Winning at Work Means Losing at Life: A Book of Renewal for Leaders* J.P. Tarcher

This book draws upon psychological and business strategies to show successful business executives how to stop feeling that the pain of success outweighs the rewards.

Blanchard K.H. & Edington D.W. (1999) *The One Minute Manager Balances Work and Life* One Minute Manager Library, William Morrow, now HarperCollins, New York.

This book is in the familiar One Minute Manager format, but deals with the personal issue of getting your life in balance. The One Minute Manager finds himself overwhelmed by success, and wakes up with chest pains. Many people are frightened by such an experience, but soon revert to their old behaviors. This book shows ways to improve all aspects of life by starting with eating healthier foods and exercising in the right ways. The book encourages us each to focus on tone, perspective, connectedness, and autonomy as ways to create a satisfying and rewarding life.

Anderson R., Anderson J., Kahn L. (ed) (1997) *Stretching at Your Computer or Desk* Shelter Publishing, Ashland, Ohio.

Bob Anderson has been spreading the gospel of flexibility for decades (he first published *Stretching* in 1980; it has two million copies in print in 17 languages), and now he applies what he knows to the modern keyboard culture. The exercises in this book are designed for workplace settings - sitting at your desk, standing at the copy machine, talking on the phone - and can all be done without drawing too much attention to yourself. People with lower-back, neck and shoulder pain from sitting too much, or with repetitive stress injuries from typing, will find this book especially useful.

Bonomo P., Seidler D., & Piser J. (illustrator) (1998)
ErgAerobics: Why does working @ my computer hurt so much? **ErgAerobics Inc., New York.**

This is a comprehensive guide to help computer users prevent and treat Computer-Induced Repetitive Stress Injuries (CIRSIs) such as carpal tunnel syndrome, back pain, neck pain, and headaches. Computer use has dramatically increased in the last ten years with no sign of decline in sight. With increased use, the likelihood of a computer user experiencing one or more CIRSIs is greater. Everyone knows someone who has had carpal tunnel syndrome or severe back pain. The US Department of Labor estimates that one half of the workforce will experience a repetitive stress injury at some point in a normal career. You may or may not feel the effects yet, but chances are that after years, or even just months of computer use, you will become a victim too. Learn the signs to watch for and the mistakes to avoid.

WEBSITES

Healthy People

Healthy People is a US prevention agenda for the nation. It is a statement of national opportunities – a tool that identifies the most significant preventable threats to health and focuses public and private sector efforts to address those threats. Healthy People offers a simple but powerful idea: provide the information and knowledge about how to improve health in a format that enables diverse groups to combine their efforts and work as a team. It is a road map to better health for all that can be used by many different people, states and communities, businesses, professional organizations, groups whose concern is a particular threat to health, or a particular population group. Healthy People is based on scientific knowledge and is used for decision making and for action.

The first set of national health targets was published in 1979 in *Healthy People: The Surgeon General's Report on Health Promotion and Disease Prevention*. This set of five challenging goals, to reduce mortality among four age groups – infants, children, adolescents and young adults, and adults – and increase independence among older adults, was supported by objectives with 1990 targets that drove the action.

Healthy People 2000 was released in 1990 to follow on from the original program. It is a comprehensive agenda with three overarching goals: to increase years of healthy life, to reduce disparities in health among different population groups, and to achieve access to preventive health services.

To date, 47 States, the District of Columbia, and Guam have developed their own Healthy People plans. Most states have emulated national objectives, but virtually all have tailored them to their specific needs. Healthy People objectives have been specified by Congress as the metric for measuring the progress of the Indian Health Service, the Maternal and Child Health Block Grant, and the Preventive Health and Health Services Block Grant. Ongoing involvement is ensured through the Healthy People Consortium – an alliance of 350 national membership organizations and 300 state health, mental health, substance abuse, and environmental agencies.

For current information about the Healthy People initiative, visit the main Website at http://www.health.gov/healthypeople

The Leading Health Indicators established by Healthy People 2010 will be used to measure the health of the US over the next 10 years.

Training, Health & Fitness

This is a Website that offers pretty well everything you need to train well and stay fit. The following major sites can all be found there:

» Physiology & Injury Prevention
» Fitness Friday
» The future of physical fitness
» Exceptional Americans getting old and staying fit
» Our consuming passion for energy foods
» Training programmes
» Arthritis Foundation: Dublin Marathon – Training Program
» Katherine Switzer: A Walking and Running program for all abilities
» John Barbour: Marathon Training Program
» Glenn Chaple: 5M/5K Training Program
» Health and Fitness Forum

» Training – Health & Fitness Forum
» Cool Running Training and Fitness Editorials
» David Hampson: Run Faster And Easier With Better Economy
» David Hampson: VO2 max: What is it, Why is it so important, and how do you improve it?
» Dr Richard Hawkins: Kneecap Pain In Runners.

The Office of Disease Prevention and Health Promotion (ODPHP)

The Office of Public Health and Science, Office of the Secretary, US Department of Health and Human Services, works to strengthen the disease prevention and health promotion priorities of the Department within the collaborative framework of the HHS agencies. Details are available on its Website http://odphp.osophs.dhhs.gov/

Other sites maintained by the ODPHP include

» Community Implementation Micro-Grants for Healthy People 2010
» Surgeon General Releases New Site Especially For Kids
» Nutrition and Your Health: Dietary Guidelines for Americans, 2000.

Publications on-line

» Healthy People 2010 (November 2000)
» Nutrition and Your Health: Dietary Guidelines for Americans, Fifth Edition
» Prevention Report
» 2001 Federal Health Information Centers and Clearinghouses, 2001 National Health Observances, *and* 2001 Toll-Free Numbers for Health Information
» Wired for Health and Well-Being: The Emergence of Interactive Health Communication
» Guide to Clinical Preventive Services, Second Edition
» Clinician's Handbook of Preventive Services, Second Edition.

Other Internet sites supported by ODPHP

» Commission on Dietary Supplement Labels
» Environmental Health Policy Committee

» Families and Children Section, US State & Local Government Gateway
» Health Section, US State & Local Government Gateway
» healthfinder®
» Healthy People 2010
» Healthy People 2000 Initiative
» HHS Partner Gateway
» National Health Information Center
» Partnerships for Networked Consumer Health Information
» Public Health Functions Project
» US–Russian Health Committee
» www.health.gov
» www.surgeongeneral.gov

A Healthy Me.com

This site is produced by Blue Cross Blue Shield of Massachusetts (BCBSMA) for use by anyone who is interested in keeping themselves and their loved ones healthy.

It is designed to provide immediate, open access to information on the health issues that are important to you – at the moment they become important to you. You can receive the latest news and information on fitness, nutrition, parenting, women's health, pregnancy, alternative health, and more. You can even tailor ahealthyme.com to suit your individual needs, and receive personalized e-mail updates. You can search the extensive database of medical journals and consumer publications for articles of interest: full-text versions are published on the site when available. You can also shop online for health-related products, books, and more.

Blue Cross Blue Shield work closely with Consumer Health Interactive, a San Francisco-based company which develops customized Websites for major healthcare companies. It has created hundreds of original stories on health topics, health tools and quizzes, a health encyclopaedia and drug and herb databases, shopping partnerships, health plan information, and thousands of news and journal articles on the latest in health and medicine. For more information, check out CHI's Website at www.consumerhi.com

Multum

Multum is a leading provider of drug information and tools. Based in Denver, Colorado, it was founded in 1992 to combat medication errors, which claim the lives of up to 7000 Americans each year. At Multum, physicians and pharmacists work with software engineers and others to create current, comprehensive drug information for medical professionals and consumers. By searching Multum's database, you can get up-to-date research information on the benefits, risks, and side effects of drugs, and on their interactions with other drugs.

The Natural Pharmacist

The herbal index created by The Natural Pharmacist features one of the most comprehensive encyclopaedias on herbs and supplements available. As TNP explains, "We cut through the hype to tell you what is known and what remains to be proven regarding popular natural treatments. Setting a new, high standard of accuracy and objectivity, this site takes a realistic look at the herbs and supplements you hear about in the news. You will encounter both favorable and unfavorable studies and learn about the benefits and risks of natural treatments." The Natural Pharmacist is science-based, easy to understand, independent, and overseen by physicians; it tells you not only about herbs' safety and effectiveness, but their possible side effects and interactions with other herbs and drugs. Engaging, balanced, and well-written, it is an invaluable resource for every consumer interested in learning more about integrative medicine.

The PDR Family Guide Encyclopaedia of Medical Care

What are the most important steps to take after your doctor's visit? PDR's Family Guide Encyclopaedia of Medical Care will help you find that out. Published by Medical Economics, one of the leading publishers of medical magazines and directories, this guide gives you in-depth information on hundreds of common medical problems and treatments – plus instructions on self-care after seeing the doctor. In addition, it tells you what to expect during and after clinic visits and hospitalization, as well as crucial warning signs of emergencies and complications that need immediate medical attention.

ProQuest Information and Learning,

ProQuest Information and Learning has its headquarters in Ann Arbor, Michigan, and is one of the leading distributors of online journals and magazines in the US. Among the magazines and journals it carries are Child Health Alert, the American Journal of Sports Medicine, Diabetes Forecast, The Lancet, Nutrition Action Health Information Newsletter, and Paediatrics for Parents.

Reuters Health

Reuters Health is the premier wire service delivering daily health and medical news world-wide. Its health news is distributed to over 200 Websites in more than 20 countries around the globe. It delivers cutting-edge stories on men's, women's, and children's health, as well as the latest research on diet and exercise, new treatments, and disease management.

Health and Fitness.com

Health and Fitness Online (H&F) is an alliance of professionals contributing to a multi-media production of fitness information, resources, products and services. Through its website, H&F promotes and inspires a healthy lifestyle approach to fitness that is applicable to all audiences. This is an up-to-date, reliable resource, emphasizing fitness as it relates to health, in an entertaining and interactive presentation.

work-and-health.org

Work and health is an emerging field that examines relationships between employment experiences and health status. This is a broad, interdisciplinary territory that crosses many fields of study, including public health, psychology, sociology, anthropology, medicine, social welfare, economics, and business.

Unemployment, job loss, and work stress all affect health. More recently, the changing nature of work may also have health conse-quences. Job security is less common, and more jobs are temporary without benefits. Researchers, policy makers, community practitioners, and journalists are paying increasing attention to these issues. The

Work and Health Map on this site provides information about relevant research studies, organizations, websites, and people who are contributing to our knowledge about the connections between work and health. Summaries of important recent studies in a variety of topic areas are included.

The map draws together many of the disparate areas of study contributing to knowledge about employment and health and organizes them into four different categories of relationships contributing to a field of work and health. There are advantages to defining a field of work and health that draws from many disciplines:

1 Linking work and health can affect policy-making strategies. Work and health are typically not linked in public perception. Yet programs to enhance people's work opportunities and those to provide health services consume tremendous public and private resources.

2 What makes a job health promoting? Some jobs enhance health and others may not. Disseminating information about the ingredients of health-promoting jobs may in itself be an important health promotion activity.

3 Opportunities for collaborative projects. Concentrating on the connections between work and health could promote collaborative projects between professionals. For example, public health is a multidisciplinary field including epidemiologists, bio-statisticians, toxicologists, health educators, and others working together. The field of work and health could function similarly.

Ten Steps to Making Body Care Work

1 Check the working environment
  » The work-station
  » The environment
  » The building fabric
  » The building maintenance
2 Check current health status
3 Set health goals
4 Check the diet
5 Look at exercise
6 Look at lifestyle
  » Meditation
  » Spiritual conviction
  » A support system
7 Stress
8 Self care
9 Long-term health and body care
10 Work and leisure.

Go jogging, it will add years to your life. Doctors at Bispebjerg University Hospital in Denmark conducted a 22-year study of 5000 men and found that jogging for just two hours a week can reduce the likelihood of premature death by 60%. The benefits of the regular jogging are thought to take effect almost immediately. Studies have shown that running improves circulation, strengthens the heart muscles and may even protect against cancer.

Throughout this book we have looked at pretty well all the aspects necessary for any manager to:

» implement a body care program for the team; and
» implement a personal body care program.

To condense this information down into Ten Easy Steps to body care, we can look at:

» checking our working environment;
» checking our current health status;
» setting health goals;
» checking our diet;
» exercise;
» lifestyle;
» stress;
» self care;
» long-term health and body care; and
» work and leisure.

1. CHECK THE WORKING ENVIRONMENT

We need to check four areas here:

» our immediate work area – work-station, desk, bench, whatever;
» our immediate environment – the office in which our work-station is situated;
» the fabric of the building in which we work; and
» the maintenance of the building in which we work.

Of course this list assumes we all work in offices, but even if we do not, the same principles apply.

The work-station

This is our immediate area of work, that bit which we use most each day. We need to check that it is physically comfortable, safe, and beneficial. See Chapter 4 for more details.

The environment

We need to check that the place around our own work-station is also safe and healthy. We need to be aware both for ourselves and for others of any potential dangers from faulty apparatus and equipment as well as dangers from hazards.

The building fabric

This applies no matter where we work. No employer should expect us to work in an unsafe environment and we need to watch out for potential dangers to our health from unsafe elevators, faulty window catches, loose floor covering, damaged railings on stairwells – that sort of thing. Report any defects immediately to a health and safety executive.

The building maintenance

You need to be on the lookout for potential dangers and hazards to your health from such things as dangerous chemicals being stored, faulty air conditioning units – that sort of thing.

2. CHECK CURRENT HEALTH STATUS

How healthy are we now? It is essential to have regular medical check-ups. These should include:

» heart;
» weight;
» blood pressure;
» blood samples for analysis, including cholesterol tests;
» urinary and bowel systems; and
» smear tests for women.

We should also:

» get our hearing tested from time to time;
» visit a dentist every six months;

» make sure our inoculations are up to date;
» get our eyes tested at least once a year, and wear any spectacles that are prescribed; and
» perform regular self-examination tests – testicles for men, women should check their breasts; keep an eye on any moles or warts – check for changes in size, color, or texture and report any changes immediately to a qualified medical practitioner.

3. SET HEALTH GOALS

We need to look at ourselves very objectively – and decide what is to be changed. If we are over- or under-weight we need to do something about it. If we do not take regular exercise we need to do something about it. If we are generally unfit and unwell we need to do something about it. These things will not put themselves right – we have to take action. We must have a plan of action, with achievable targets – get fitter in six months, lose so many pounds over the next three months, take up a regular form of exercise this summer, that sort of thing. Support and encouragement from family and friends can be a powerful factor in helping us to stick to a plan once we have started out on it.

4. CHECK THE DIET

If we do not eat right we will not be right. So what is right? The basic recommendations for a diet which will bring good health are:

» base one meal each day on raw food such as salads;
» cut down on saturated fats;
» cut down on sugar;
» drink plenty of water;
» eat four to six slices of whole-wheat bread each day;
» eat at least five portions of fruit or vegetables each day;
» eat fish instead of meat once or twice a week;
» eat less red meat;
» eat three good meals a day, rather than snacking;
» if snacks are wanted, then go for raw carrots and apples rather than chips or crisps;
» make meat an ingredient rather than the main part of the meal;

» make sure that at least a third of your diet is whole-wheat bread, pasta and cereals;
» drink no more than two or three cups of coffee in a day;
» reduce alcohol intake to the recommended levels – 18-21 units each week for men, 9-14 units per week for women. These units should be spread evenly over a week. (A unit is 10g of alcohol – half a pint of beer, one measure of spirits, one glass of wine); and
» use less salt.

5. LOOK AT EXERCISE

We all lead much more sedentary lifestyles than our grandparents did. If we do not do physical work we need to do something physical outside work to make sure we stay healthy. It is not necessary to do "exercises" to stay fit. There is a whole range of activities that will keep us fit without us ever having to turn to a gym. These activities could include:

» gardening;
» housework;
» canoeing;
» martial arts;
» brisk walking;
» dancing;
» swimming;
» sailing; or
» cycling.

If you can think of other activities, then you are well on the way to planning your own program.

6. LOOK AT LIFESTYLE

Research in the US has shown that patients recovering from heart attacks recovered quicker and were far less likely to have a subsequent attack if they fulfilled three criteria:

» they learned a meditation or relaxation technique;
» they had some form of spiritual conviction; and
» they had some form of support system.

Meditation

This does not have to mean wearing any particular costume, burning incense, or shaving your head. Learning a simple meditation technique should require no major changes in lifestyle and no expense, just sitting quietly, and still, once a day and turning off the incessant chatter of the mind.

Spiritual conviction

Having a spiritual conviction does not mean joining an organized religion, it simply involves working out, for yourself, a satisfactory explanation of the universe and all that is in it, and being at ease with your own position within the world.

A support system

Joining an evening class, having friends round to supper, being part of a charity or club, having relatives nearby – all these are support systems. It does not seem to matter what the support system is, just so long as we have someone around us to chat to, to share our worries with. Contact with other people – real contact, not phone-calls, e-mails, or pen-pals – is a very important part of helping us to be comfortable with ourselves. We need to have a shoulder to cry on if necessary, someone to talk to about something other than work – it is all important in having a balanced lifestyle.

We need to look at our lifestyle and see if it is supporting us, keeping us healthy, or if it is likely to cause us ill health in the long term. Living to work is not the answer. Working to live is.

7. STRESS

Job dissatisfaction is bad for your health, according to Professor Cary Cooper, BUPA Professor of Organizational Psychology and Health at the University of Manchester Institute of Science and Technology (UMIST) in the UK. Cooper's research indicates that 30 million working days are lost each year in the UK through stress. Dr James Lefanu agreed; male patients who answered negatively to enquiries about work were often found to be suffering from headaches, palpitations or sleeping difficulties. "This distress poses a much more significant threat to the physical and mental well-being of young men than virtually everything else combined," he says.

So what causes job dissatisfaction? Often it is because we are exhausted. We feel depressed and finding the strength and resolve to carry on is often hard. If we look at our body care practices we might well find that improving our diet, taking more regular exercise, and getting better quality sleep will all help us to improve the situation for ourselves.

If we monitor our stress levels, we get a pretty good idea how our physical machinery is functioning – too much stress and bits are likely to break down, not enough stress and we sink into depression and apathy – just the right amount and we thrive.

When we wish to counteract the effects of stress in our lives we have to take various steps. Initially we have to *recognize the signs*. These may include insomnia, panic attacks, weight loss, trembling, new phobias, irritable bowel syndrome, palpitations, irritability, hyperventilation, muscular tension especially around the neck and shoulders, headaches including migraines, addiction problems, high blood pressure, an over-fast pulse, and unfounded anxieties. Some of these symptoms will obviously be more serious than others and will, to a certain degree, indicate the ability to channel and process stress.

Once we have recognized the signs and realized that we are suffering from a badly processed response to stress, we have to *identify the causes*. Stress management consultants work with a general list of about 45 principal life events that are known to cause stress. These are shown in Table 10.1. Each of these causes has a rating, and they range from the death of a spouse (rated at 100), to a rise in mortgage rates (rated as 31), and a minor breaking of the law (rated as 15). If you build up a score of more than 150 in a year, the chances are that you will experience a down-turn in health of some sort. A score of anything over 300 in one year will almost certainly lead to major health problems unless action is taken.

Knowing what is on the list is helpful; it can enable us to plan in advance how many of the major changes within our own control we will make in one year.

8. SELF CARE

If you have any doubts about your body, then consult a qualified medical practitioner immediately. This is one area where you simply cannot afford to procrastinate.

Table 10.1 Causes of stress and their relative ratings.

Cause of stress	Rating
Death of a spouse	100
Divorce	75
Death of someone close in the family, marital separation, or a prison sentence	all 65
Serious injury or illness	55
Getting married	50
Redundancy or dismissal	48
Marital reconciliation	45
Retirement, or illness affecting a close family member	both 44
Pregnancy, or sexual difficulties	40
A new baby	39
Death of close friend, change in business or in financial affairs	all 38
Change in work	37
Change in relationship with partner	36
Mortgage rate rise	31
Loss of mortgage	30
New boss	28
Children leaving home	27
Winning an award, or problems with in-laws	both 26
Partner changing type of work	25
Beginning or stopping study course, or change in living conditions	both 23
Change in personal habits	22
Falling out with boss	21
Change in working conditions, or moving house	both 20
Children changing schools	19
Change in social activities or religious activities	both 18
Taking out a loan, or altered sleeping habits	both 17
Change in family location	16
Dieting, holidays, Christmas, and minor law-breaking	all 15

If you notice any of the following signs seek medical advice at once:

» blood in the faeces;
» blood in the urine;
» bruises without any obvious injury;
» coughing up blood;
» lumps in the breast;
» persistent difficulty swallowing;
» persistent headaches;
» persistent white patches in the mouth;
» rectal bleeding;
» recurrent hoarseness;
» recurrent abdominal pain;
» sores or scabs that refuse to heal;
» testicular abnormalities;
» unexplained constipation and/or diarrhoea; or
» unexplained weight loss.

9. LONG-TERM HEALTH AND BODY CARE

As we get older, the system starts to go wrong, to break down, and to need repairing more often. Long-term health care means constant maintenance, putting things right at once before they get worse, and regular check-ups. It also means being kind to ourselves and not pushing ourselves harder than we can stand. What we can do at the age of twenty is a lot more than what we can do when we are fifty. It is natural to ease off as we get older, just so long as we do not give up altogether. The three principal factors necessary for helping us to survive into a long, healthy, and productive old age are regular exercise, a healthy diet, and not smoking.

10. WORK AND LEISURE

There are five key points about getting the home/work balance right:

» have other interests apart from your work to keep you vital and interesting;
» realize that your leisure activities are recharging your system and keeping you healthy for work – they are essential for you to be able to work productively;

» separate work from home, and keep them separate;
» stop work when you are supposed to and enjoy some leisure time; and
» remember that money you earn from work is for leisure activities just as much as it is for paying bills – have a life, and have a good one.

Frequently Asked Questions (FAQs)

Q1: How does body care affect an employee's productivity and what are the benefits of keeping employees healthy?

A: See Chapter 1.

Q2: What is body care and what sorts of conditions does it cover?

A: See Chapter 2.

Q3: Why is there such an emphasis on body care in the modern workplace?

A: See Chapter 3.

Q4: How do we go about implementing safe and healthy working practices in the office?

A: See Chapter 4.

Q5: What do we know about the work/home balance and how it affects the overall health of employees?

A: See Chapter 5.

Q6: What is the current thinking about body care and work related illnesses?

A: See Chapter 6.

Q7: How do we, as individuals, put good body care into practice?

A: See Chapter 7.

Q8: What are the key concepts about body care that I ought to know about?

A: See Chapter 8.

Q9: Where do I go if I want more information and resources for body care?

A: See Chapter 9.

Q10: What are the ten steps to making body care work?

A: See Chapter 10.

Index